EAT CALIFORNIA

Vibrant recipes
from the West Coast

Vivian Lui

Photography by Con Poulos

Smith
Street
Books

CONTENTS

INTRODUCTION

It's safe to say California has a lot going for it: snow-capped mountains, golden beaches, and just as enticingly, a vibrant food culture. The seafood is fresh, the meat is beyond organic and happily raised, and the farmers' markets are a wealth of riches all year round. Thanks to the coastal state's fertile soil and temperate climate, local produce is varied and abundant, from the famed citrus to the beloved avocado. California is so lush that even wild fennel grows out of cracks in empty car parks. In the same way that California's landscape cultivates incredible produce, it also inspires a lifestyle of movement and wellness. Where else in the world can you hit the ski slopes in the morning, break for a grain bowl and a green juice, and still make it to the beach for a sunset surf session?

Californians take none of this for granted – they hold a deep appreciation for the land, the harvest it yields and the nourishment it provides. Which is why local farmers' markets, where berries spill out of baskets and bunches of kale are piled high, are a weekly destination for chefs and home cooks alike. It's where ingredients are explored and dishes are inspired by the bounty that different seasons bring. The arrival of kumquats indicates winter; broad (fava) beans mean spring is in the air; with summer comes corn and kabocha squash signals the start of autumn. Along with this plentitude comes the great culinary delight of discovering something new about a familiar ingredient. It can be as simple as sautéing purslane instead of eating it raw or realising the skin of a particular type of avocado is edible.

But the impressive range of fresh and local produce isn't the only element that influences Californian cooking. The state's cultural diversity means finding vendors hawking handmade tacos next to a bustling Korean BBQ restaurant, both just steps away from a food truck that fuses them together to create something completely new. The food scene offers an abundance of flavours and techniques, and Californians appreciate them all. It is this genuine love of food – preparing it, eating it and sharing it – that fuels this positive energy in kitchens and around tables, and makes California truly golden.

BREAKFAST & BRUNCH

They say breakfast is the most important meal of the day, and the recipes here will help you treat it as such. Simple yet tasty dishes – such as a fruit-topped smoothie bowl or granola packed with seeds and nuts – are the perfect way to start a weekday; prepping them the night before leaves plenty of time in the morning. If breakfast is the most important, brunch is the most relished. Every bite of updated classics such as crisp chilaquiles and blackberry cornmeal pancakes should be savoured – especially while sitting outside soaking up all the Californian sunshine.

AVOCADO GROVES

Due to optimal weather and soil conditions, California is the largest producer of avocados in the US at about 90 per cent. Discovered in Southern California, the Hass variety is the most ubiquitous avocado. However, during peak season more than 10 types are available at farmers' markets, including one with an edible peel. Treasured for their rich flavour and good fats, there are a variety of ways to prepare avocados: grill halves on the barbecue, purée it for a dressing or simply grab a spoon and eat it right out of the skin.

AVOCADO TOAST

Avocado toast may have been a passing trend for some but the fruit is synonymous with California. It's the perfect canvas to add different textures and flavours so be playful with other topping choices.

4 large eggs

2 medium avocados, halved, stoned, peeled and sliced

4 large or 8 small slices good bread, such as seeded loaf, country or sourdough, toasted

Sea salt flakes and freshly ground black pepper

6 radishes, very finely sliced

20 g (¾ oz) mixed sprouts

20 g (¾ oz) hemp seeds

Extra virgin olive oil, for drizzling

serves 4   **prep** 10 mins   **cook** 10 mins

Bring a small pan of water to the boil. Use enough water to cover 4 eggs by 2.5 cm (1 in). Lower the eggs into the water and simmer for 7 minutes. Transfer the eggs to an ice bath. Gently crack the eggs all around and leave to cool just enough to handle. Peel and slice the eggs.

Divide the avocado slices evenly among the toast. Season lightly with salt and pepper. Top with egg and season again. Garnish with the radishes, sprouts, hemp seeds, a drizzle of olive oil and top with a final sprinkle of salt and pepper.

SUNRISE CHIA SMOOTHIE BOWL

There are Californian eateries that strictly focus on bowls. This version combines the freshness of a smoothie with the creaminess of a chia pudding. Creating your own bowl at home allows you to hone your design skills with the myriad of toppings.

1 tablespoon chia seeds

170 ml (5½ fl oz/⅔ cup) nut (see page 55), seed or coconut milk

½ banana, sliced

100 g (3½ oz) mixed berries

1 teaspoon grated ginger

Grated zest of 1 lime

Pinch of sea salt flakes

Toppings:

Sliced seasonal fruit, chopped nuts, toasted coconut, ground linseeds (flax seeds)

serves 1   **prep** 5 mins + overnight chilling & freezing   **cook** none

Place the chia seeds and 60 ml (2 fl oz/¼ cup) of the milk in a small container and stir to combine, then chill in the fridge overnight.

Lay a piece of plastic wrap or greaseproof paper in a soup bowl. Add the banana and berries to the bowl and freeze overnight. The frozen bowl will keep your breakfast perfectly chilled and the frozen berries will lend a good consistency.

In the morning, add the chia mixture, remaining milk, the frozen fruit, ginger, lime zest and salt to a blender and process until smooth. Transfer to the frozen bowl and enjoy with toppings of choice.

BREAKFAST TACOS

Tacos come in many forms throughout California – traditional versions from trucks, Korean tacos and vegan tacos with jicama as the base. The tortilla is a perfect vessel to fill with different ingredients, so it makes sense that there are so many adaptations.

4 tablespoons extra virgin olive oil

230 g (8 oz) fresh breakfast sausage, casings removed

1 small onion, finely sliced

1 large poblano chilli pepper, stemmed, seeded and sliced

Sea salt flakes and freshly ground black pepper

1 garlic clove, grated

8 small corn tortillas (about 13 cm/5 in in diameter)

8 large eggs

Toppings:

Sliced jalapeño, pickled radish (see page 209) and coriander (cilantro) leaves

serves 4 **prep** 5 mins **cook** 25 mins

Heat a large non-stick frying pan over medium–high heat. Add 1 tablespoon of the olive oil and the sausage and cook for 6–8 minutes, breaking up the sausage with a wooden spoon and stirring frequently, until the meat is browned. Transfer to a bowl and set aside.

Add another tablespoon of the oil to the pan, then add the onion and cook for 3 minutes, or until translucent. Add the poblano chilli pepper and season. Cook for 5 minutes, or until the vegetables begin to caramelise. Add the garlic and cook for another minute. Transfer to the bowl with the sausage. Wipe out the pan and set aside.

Meanwhile, toast the tortillas over a direct flame for 1 minute, or until lightly charred in spots or to desired doneness. Flip and repeat. Transfer to a plate and cover with a dish towel to keep warm.

Crack the eggs into a medium bowl, season and whisk. Return the frying pan to medium–high heat. Add the remaining 2 tablespoons of oil and swirl to coat. Pour in the eggs and immediately reduce the heat to medium–low. Fold gently a few times and tilt the pan to allow any very runny parts to cook. Continue until mostly set with large billowy curds, about 3–4 minutes. Remove the pan from the heat.

To serve, divide the eggs onto the tortillas. Top with the sausage mixture and finish with desired toppings.

CHILAQUILES

Originally a traditional Mexican breakfast, this crispier, Californian version is not simmered in the salsa as found in many regions throughout Mexico. Customise to your liking with refried beans, shredded chicken or even sautéed vegetables.

450 g (1 lb) tomatoes, halved

1 small onion, quartered

1 jalapeño chilli, stemmed, halved and seeded if you like less heat

1 garlic clove, unpeeled

2 chipotles in adobo, plus 2 tablespoons of liquid

Sea salt flakes and freshly ground black pepper

Rapeseed or neutral oil, for frying

250 g (9 oz) small corn tortillas, quartered

8 large eggs

2 tablespoons extra virgin olive oil

85 g (3 oz) cotija cheese or firm feta, crumbled

1 avocado, sliced

2 spring (green) onions, chopped

6 small radishes, finely sliced

serves 4   **prep** 10 mins   **cook** 20 mins

Preheat the griller (broiler) with the rack 15 cm (6 in) from the top. Place the tomatoes, onion, jalapeño and garlic in a cast-iron frying pan and grill for 10–12 minutes until slightly charred in spots, flipping the vegetables once, halfway through. Squeeze the garlic clove out of its skin, discarding the skin. Transfer the vegetables to a food processor or blender, add the chipotles and liquid, season and purée until just smooth. Cover to keep warm.

Meanwhile, heat 7 cm (2¾ in) rapeseed oil in a large heavy casserole dish until it reaches 180°C (350°F). Fry the tortillas in 2 batches for 2–3 minutes, flipping once until golden and crispy. Transfer to a baking sheet lined with kitchen paper and season lightly with salt.

Crack the eggs into a medium bowl, season and whisk. Heat a large non-stick frying pan over medium–high heat. Add the olive oil and swirl to coat. Pour in the eggs and immediately reduce the heat to medium–low. Fold gently a few times and tilt the pan to allow any very runny parts to cook. Continue until mostly set with large billowy curds, about 3–4 minutes. Remove the pan from the heat.

Place the tortilla chips onto 4 plates. Ladle the sauce over and divide the eggs between the plates. Top with the cheese, avocado, spring onion and radish.

Note: Making home-made tortilla chips makes a difference but in a pinch, buy thick corn tortilla chips if you are not up for frying your own.

BAKED EGGS WITH FORAGED GREENS & HERBS

A take on shakshuka, this utilises the various greens growing in California in a different way than just salad – foraged from the wild or a farmers' market. The herbs add another layer of freshness to the cooked vegetables.

2 tablespoons unsalted butter

3 tablespoons extra virgin olive oil, plus extra for drizzling

2 small leeks, chopped

Sea salt flakes and freshly ground black pepper

300 g (10½ oz) mixed foraged greens, such as mustard greens, watercress, purslane and rocket (arugula), chopped

375 g (13 oz) mixed cherry tomatoes, halved if large

30 g (1 oz) parmesan cheese, grated, plus extra to serve

1 teaspoon sumac

8 large eggs

2 handfuls of mixed wild herbs or flowers, such as chervil, wild fennel, mustard flowers, radish flowers

4 thick slices good-quality crusty bread, toasted, to serve

serves 4   **prep** 5 mins   **cook** 20 mins

Preheat the oven to 200°C (400°F).

Place a large cast-iron frying pan over medium heat. (It should be large enough to fit 8 eggs.) Add the butter, 1 tablespoon of the olive oil, the leeks and season. Cook for 5 minutes until softened. Add the remaining 2 tablespoons olive oil and stir in the mixed greens in 2 batches to wilt, about 1 minute each, and season. Add the tomatoes, cheese and half the sumac and stir to combine.

Make 8 wells and crack the eggs into them. Transfer the pan to the oven and bake for 10–12 minutes until the whites are just set, rotating the pan once halfway through. Top with a drizzle of olive oil, then sprinkle with the remaining sumac, the herbs or flowers and cheese, if liked. Season and serve immediately with bread.

SURF

Surf culture permeates the Golden State, thanks to its idyllic location on the edge of the Pacific. Whether sharing a party wave or admiring an old timer's restored VW van, the good vibes of the surf community are palpable in the water and on the shore. You will find young and old, beginners and experts, longboarders and shortboarders alike – everyone is there to have a good time and relish the grandeur of the ocean. There's nothing like a surf session to make you feel famished (even when you are just watching from the shore), so the next stop is undoubtedly somewhere to refuel.

SURFER'S BREAKFAST

A simple but delicious breakfast that relies on high-quality ingredients, this dish makes for a perfect post-surf meal – one that you can quickly put together even when camping at the beach.

8 thick-cut bacon slices (about 340 g/12 oz)

2 small avocados, halved and stoned

8 large eggs

4 English muffins, split and toasted

Salted butter, to serve

Fermented Hot Sauce (see page 213), to serve (optional)

Sea salt flakes and freshly ground black pepper

serves 4   **prep** none   **cook** 25 mins

Arrange the bacon in a single layer in a large cast-iron frying pan. Place the pan over medium heat and cook for 10–12 minutes, flipping once halfway through, until the fat is rendered and the bacon is golden and crispy. Adjust the heat on the second side if the pan gets too hot and starts to smoke. Transfer the bacon to a plate lined with kitchen paper.

Pour out all but 1 tablespoon of the fat and set aside. Return the pan to medium heat, place the avocados, cut side down, in the pan and cook for 1–2 minutes until browned. Set the avocados aside.

Increase the heat to medium high. Crack 4 eggs into the pan and reduce the heat to low after 1 minute. Cook for another 3 minutes, or until the edges are browned and crispy and the whites have just set, or until desired doneness. Transfer the eggs to a plate, then return the frying pan to medium–high heat and add 1 tablespoon of the reserved bacon fat. Repeat with the remaining eggs.

Serve 2 eggs, 2 bacon rashers, an avocado half, English muffins, butter and hot sauce, if using, and season to taste.

CALIFORNIA GRAIN BOWL

Grain bowls are a popular way to showcase heirloom grains and farmers' market bounty. They have become a staple at many eateries throughout California. This breakfast version is a cosy way to start the day but is suitable for lunch or dinner.

125 g (4½ oz) buckwheat

135 g (5 oz) rye grains

1.15 litres (38 fl oz) vegetable stock (see page 197)

4 tablespoons extra virgin olive oil

Sea salt flakes

4 large eggs

1 shallot, finely sliced

225 g (8 oz) mixed mushrooms, sliced

170 g (6 oz) spinach, thick stems removed

150 g (5½ oz) pickles (see page 209)

serves 4   **prep** 10 mins + overnight soaking
cook 50 mins

Soak the grains overnight. They can be soaked together. The next morning, drain the grains and shake off any excess liquid.

Bring the stock to a simmer in a small saucepan. Reduce the heat to low to keep warm.

Heat a large sauté pan over medium heat. Add 2 tablespoons of the olive oil and stir in the grains to coat. Add 1 teaspoon salt and a ladleful of stock. Stir frequently for 5 minutes until almost all the liquid is absorbed. Add another ladleful of stock and repeat until all the stock is used up, about 30–35 minutes. The mixture will be slightly creamy but still have a little bite from the rye grains. Turn off the heat and cover. A splash of water can be added to reheat just before serving.

While the grains are cooking, bring a small saucepan of water to the boil. Use enough water to cover 4 eggs by 2.5 cm (1 in). Lower the eggs into the water and simmer for 6 minutes. Transfer the eggs to an ice bath. Gently crack the eggs all around and leave to cool just enough to handle. Peel and set the eggs aside.

Heat a large frying pan over medium–high heat. Add the remaining 2 tablespoons olive oil, the shallot, mushrooms, ½ teaspoon salt and ¼ teaspoon pepper and cook for 5–8 minutes until the mushrooms are golden. Stir in the spinach to wilt. Season lightly.

Divide the grains among 4 bowls and serve with the eggs, vegetables and pickles.

HAM & EGG BREAKFAST SANDWICH

Breakfast sandwiches are satisfying because they are little packages that deliver a lot of flavour. This meets all the notes – sweet, creamy, nutty, fresh and spicy.

2 tablespoons extra virgin olive oil

8 good-quality ham slices

40 g (1½ oz) unsalted butter, plus extra to serve

4 large eggs

75 g (2¾ oz) cheddar cheese, grated

4 bagels, split and toasted

½ bunch dandelion greens or other greens, trimmed

Fermented Hot Sauce (see page 213), to serve (optional)

Sea salt flakes and freshly ground black pepper

serves 4   **prep** none   **cook** 10 mins

Heat a large cast-iron frying pan over medium–high heat. Add 1 tablespoon of the olive oil and fry the ham for 1 minute on each side, or until crispy and browned in some spots. Remove the ham and set aside.

Return the pan to medium–high heat. Add 1 tablespoon each of the butter and olive oil, then add the eggs and cook for 1 minute. Reduce the heat. Scatter the cheese on top and cover. Cook for another 2–3 minutes until the edges of the eggs are browned and crispy, the whites have just set and the cheese has melted, or until desired doneness. Remove the pan from the heat.

Spread a little butter on the base of the bagels. Top with the ham, cheesy eggs, greens and hot sauce, if liked. Season, close the sandwich and serve.

PORRIDGE WAFFLES & STONE FRUIT

The contrast of the crispy outside to the porridge-like inside has a nice duality to this breakfast. It will also make your gluten-free guests happy.

100 g (3½ oz/½ cup) quinoa

90 g (3 oz/1 cup) Scottish oats or quick cooking steel-cut oats

1 teaspoon sea salt

120 g (4½ oz) oat flour

4 teaspoons baking powder

2 teaspoons ground ginger

4 large eggs, separated

400 ml (13½ fl oz) can unsweetened coconut milk

60 ml (2 fl oz/¼ cup) maple syrup, plus extra to serve (optional)

60 g (2½ oz) butter, melted and slighly cooled, plus extra for greasing

Toppings:

160 ml (5½ fl oz) coconut cream

Sliced stone fruit, toasted black sesame seeds, toasted hazelnuts

serves 4   **prep** 10 mins   **cook** 40 mins
equipment Belgian waffle maker

Preheat the oven to 110°C (230°F) with a wire rack set inside a baking sheet.

Toast the quinoa in a small saucepan over medium heat for 3–5 minutes, or until fragrant. Stir in the steel-cut oats, 350 ml (12 fl oz) water and the salt, then cover and simmer for 15 minutes. Transfer to a large plate and cool to room temperature.

Whisk the oat flour, baking powder and ground ginger together in a small bowl. Set aside.

Whisk the egg whites in a medium bowl until soft peaks form. Set aside.

Add the egg yolks, coconut milk, maple syrup and butter to a stand mixer fitted with a paddle attachment and mix on medium speed for 1 minute, or until well combined. Add the cooled quinoa and oat mixture and mix for another minute, or until just combined. Scrape down the side of the bowl, add the oat flour mixture and mix on low for 1 minute, or until just combined. Remove the bowl and gently fold in the egg whites until just incorporated.

Preheat and grease a waffle maker according to manufacturer's instructions. Add 250 ml (8½ fl oz/1 cup) of batter, or suggested amount according to the maker, and cook for 7–8 minutes until golden brown and crispy. Place the finished waffle in the oven on the rack to keep warm. Repeat with remaining batter to make 4–5, depending on the size of maker.

Serve the waffles with a spoonful of coconut cream, fruit, seeds, nuts and maple syrup, if liked.

MORNING GRANOLA

Balancing out this beautifully textured granola is creamy yoghurt and chopped seasonal fruit, which combined makes a wholesome breakfast. It's easy to store and transport as a snack on the go as well.

---

180 g (6½ oz) rolled oats

160 g (5½ oz) sunflower seeds

80 g (2¾ oz) pumpkin seeds

65 g (2¼ oz) blanched hazelnuts, roughly chopped

60 g (2 oz) shelled pistachios

60 g (2 oz) pecans, roughly chopped

50 g (1¾ oz) amaranth

40 g (1½ oz) hemp seeds

110 g (4 oz) coconut oil

50 g (1¾ oz) light brown sugar

85 g (3 oz) honey

1 teaspoon sea salt flakes

makes 1.15 litres (39 fl oz)   **prep** 5 mins
cook 1 hour + 2 hours to cool

Preheat the oven to 150°C (300°F).

Combine the oats, sunflower seeds, pumpkin seeds, nuts, amaranth and hemp seeds in a large bowl.

Place the coconut oil, sugar, honey and salt in a small saucepan over medium heat and stir for 3 minutes, or until dissolved. Add the mixture to the bowl and stir until thoroughly coated. Transfer to a baking sheet in an even layer and bake for 1 hour, stirring every 15 minutes with a large offset spatula. The mixture should be fragrant and golden brown. Turn the oven off and leave the baking sheet inside to cool completely for 2 hours. Store in an airtight container for up to 1 month.

Serve with yoghurt, Nut Milk (see page 55), fruit or even ice cream.

BANANA SEED LOAF

The seeds lend a nice crunch to this loaf. Aside from breakfast, this is also great as a midday treat, or toasted the next morning and served with salted butter.

---

110 g (4 oz) coconut oil, plus extra for greasing

190 g plain (all-purpose) flour

1½ teaspoons baking powder

½ teaspoon baking soda

1 teaspoon sea salt flakes, plus extra for sprinkling

175 g (6 oz/½ cup) honey, plus 2 tablespoons

130 g (4½ oz) smooth roasted peanut butter

2 large eggs, at room temperature, lightly whisked

1 teaspoon nautral vanilla extract

115 g (4 oz) natural yoghurt, at room temperature

60 g (2 oz) mixed seeds, such as pumpkin, sunflower, hemp and sesame

200 g (7 oz) plain chocolate (at least 70% cocoa solids), roughly chopped

3 ripe bananas, sliced

serves 6–8   **prep** 15 mins   **cook** 1 hour

Preheat the oven to 180°C (350°F).

Grease a 25 x 13 cm (10 x 5 in) loaf tin with oil, then line with baking paper to have an 8 cm (3¼ in) overhang on the sides. Lightly brush the baking paper with oil and set aside.

Whisk the flour, baking powder, baking soda and sea salt together in a bowl to combine. Set aside.

Place the coconut oil, the 175 g (6 oz/½ cup) honey and the peanut butter in a stand mixer fitted with a paddle attachment and beat on medium speed for 3 minutes, or until combined. Scrape down the sides and reduce the speed to low. Add the eggs, one at a time, stopping to scrape down after each addition. Add the vanilla and mix for another 1 minute. With the mixer on low, add half the flour mixture, the yoghurt, then the remaining flour mixture and 40 g (1½ oz) of the seeds until just combined. Remove the bowl from the stand mixer and fold in the chocolate and two-thirds of the banana by hand with a spatula. Transfer the batter to the prepared tin.

Arrange the remaining banana slices over the batter and sprinkle with the remaining 20 g (¾ oz) seeds and a light sprinkling of sea salt flakes. Lightly drizzle the remaining 2 tablespoons honey over the top and bake for 1 hour, or until a skewer comes out clean. Tent the edges for the last 15 minutes if it is getting dark. Cool for 15 minutes before lifting out of the tin to cool completely before slicing.

SKATE

Said to have begun in California in the 1950s when surfers topped a set of roller skate wheels with a piece of wood, 'sidewalk surfing' is now so much more than a way to pass the time until the waves return. That's in large part due to the fearlessness of the Z-Boys of Dogtown, a Santa Monica/Venice skate team who perfected gravity-defying tricks in the 1970s and set the stage for the skateboarding of today. From kids practising ollies and kickflips at the local skatepark to adults using skateboards as a mode of transportation, skateboarders of all types are a common sight.

POTATO PANCAKES
WITH SMOKED SALMON

The sweetness from the celeriac is a perfect base for the pops of salt from the salmon. With the rainbow of root vegetables available in California, this is a good recipe to experiment with your other favourites – beet, carrot or sweet potato.

450 g (1 lb) potatoes, such as russet, peeled

450 g (1 lb) celeriac, peeled

1 small onion, peeled

1½ teaspoons celery seeds

Sea salt flakes and freshly ground black pepper

60 g (2 oz) unsalted butter, cubed

3 tablespoons extra virgin olive oil

4 large eggs

170 g (6 oz) smoked salmon, finely sliced

60 g (2 oz) cured salmon roe

Handful of fine herbs, such as nasturtium, fennel fronds and chervil

serves 4   **prep** 15 mins   **cook** 40 mins

Use the shredder attachment of a food processor (or a box grater) to coarsely grate the potato, celeriac and onion. Place the mixture on a clean dish towel and squeeze out as much liquid as possible. Transfer to a large bowl and add the celery seeds and ½ teaspoon salt. Toss well to combine.

Heat a 25 cm (10 in) cast-iron frying pan over medium heat. Add 20 g (¾ oz) of the butter and 2 tablespoons of the olive oil. Once the butter has melted and foam has subsided, swirl the pan to coat. Add the grated potato mixture and press firmly into the pan with a flat spatula. Dot the top with the remaining butter and drizzle over the remaining olive oil. Cook for 10–15 minutes until the edges and bottom are deep brown and crisp, rotating the pan occasionally to ensure the heat is evenly distributed. Gently run a small metal spatula around the edges of the pan, then wiggle the pan back and forth to ensure that the pancake releases easily. Place a large plate over the top and carefully flip to invert the pancake onto the plate. Slide the pancake back into the pan and return to the heat, pressing to even out the pancake if needed, and repeat on the second side, cooking for another10–15 minutes. Cool on a wire rack for 5 minutes before cutting into 4 wedges.

Meanwhile, bring a medium saucepan of water to the boil. Reduce the heat to a very low simmer, then gently crack in the eggs. Poach for 3–4 minutes for medium–soft yolks. Use a slotted spoon to transfer to a plate. Lightly dab water off the bottom before serving.

Serve the pancake wedges with the poached eggs, sliced salmon, roe, herbs and lightly season.

BLACKBERRY CORNMEAL PANCAKES

Pancakes are found on many brunch menus, but can be easily made at home. It's always nice to have a bite of sweet to share at the table among the savoury dishes. The slight tartness in the blackberry complements the maple syrup in this batter.

240 ml (8 fl oz) maple syrup

290 g (10 oz) blackberries, half the amount sliced

125 g (4½ oz) plain (all-purpose) flour

45 g (1½ oz) medium-grind cornmeal

1 teaspoon baking soda

1 teaspoon sea salt

2 large eggs

225 g (8 oz) full-fat natural yoghurt

½ teaspoon natural vanilla extract

Grated zest of 1 lemon

40 g (1½ oz) unsalted butter, melted

serves 4　**prep** 5 mins　**cook** 30 mins

Preheat the oven to 100°C (210°F). Place a baking sheet with a wire rack inside to keep warm.

Place 180 ml (6 fl oz) of the maple syrup and 145 g (5 oz) whole blackberries in a small pan over low heat to warm.

Whisk the flour, cornmeal, baking soda and salt together in a large bowl. Whisk the eggs, yoghurt, the remaining maple syrup, the vanilla and lemon zest together in a medium bowl until smooth. Pour the wet mixture into the dry mixture and stir until just combined. Fold in the 145 g (5 oz) sliced blackberries.

Heat an extra-large non-stick frying pan over medium heat. Brush a thin layer of melted butter on the bottom of the pan, then drop in 60 ml (2 fl oz/¼ cup) of batter and cook for 3 minutes, or until bubbles begin to appear on the surface and the edges are golden brown. Flip and cook for another 2–3 minutes until the second side is golden brown and cooked through. Transfer to the wire rack in the oven to keep warm while making the remaining pancakes.

Serve immediately with the warmed maple syrup and berries.

DRINKS

In Californian cafes, well-crafted beverages are just as
thoughtful and inspiring as the food. It's no longer simply a
question of dairy or soy with your coffee, there's a whole range
of milks to suit your tastes, including almond, coconut, and even
oat. Flavours such as matcha and turmeric turn up on drink
menus, adding an element of wellness to your daily latte, and
you may even see shelves stacked with jars of fermenting fruit,
the colourful basis for seasonal shrubs.

MORNING GREEN SHAKE

The stereotype that it's always summer in California is not true. For gloomier days, the tropical flavours of this shake can make you feel as if you are on a sunny beach. The hemp seeds give texture and something to chew – great if this is your main breakfast.

160 g (5½ oz) chopped pineapple

160 g (5½ oz) chopped mango

60 g (2 oz) frozen coconut meat

30 g (1 oz) chopped kale

8 mint leaves

60 ml (2 fl oz/¼ cup) coconut water

Pinch of sea salt flakes

Few pinches of hemp seeds

serves 1   **prep** a few hours or overnight chilling
cook none

Chill or freeze the fruits overnight depending what texture of smoothie you prefer. Freezing will lend a lovely icy texture without having to use ice and the smoothie getting watered down.

Blend all the ingredients, except the seeds, in a high-speed blender until smooth. Top with the seeds for a slightly nutty crunch.

GOLDEN TURMERIC LATTE

Fresh turmeric root can be found at farmers' markets, speciality grocers or health food stores. Earthy and slightly floral, it has a huge range of culinary uses from adding to drinks to seasoning fish and vegetables.

---

240 ml (8 fl oz) nut (see page 55), seed or coconut milk

2 teaspoons honey

2 teaspoons dried rose petals, crushed, plus extra to garnish (optional)

20 g (¾ oz) fresh turmeric root, grated or 1 teaspoon ground

5 g (¼ oz) fresh ginger, grated

1 cardamom pod, smashed

Pinch of sea salt flakes

serves 1   **prep** 5 mins + 10 mins to cool if serving cold   **cook** 5 mins

Place all the ingredients in a small saucepan and heat gently while whisking to dissolve the honey and combine the flavours. Gently simmer on low for 5 minutes. Whisk again before straining into a mug. If serving cold, cool for at least 10 minutes, then whisk again before straining over ice. Garnish with rose petals, if liked.

MATCHA LATTE

Matcha has turned up in many culinary uses including cakes, ice creams and smoothies around California. Most commonly, this milled green tea powder is served as a tasty alternative to coffee.

1½ teaspoons matcha (green tea powder)

240 ml (8 fl oz) milk of choice, such as cow's, nut (see page 55), seed or coconut

2 teaspoons honey or kumquat syrup (see page 203)

serves 1　**prep** 5 mins　**cook** 5 mins

Place the matcha and 2 tablespoons hot but not boiling water in a measuring cup or small bowl and whisk until the matcha is fully dissolved. Transfer to a mug.

Place the milk and honey in a small saucepan and heat for 1–2 minutes until just steaming. Whisk to dissolve the honey. Remove from the heat and use a frother or whisk to froth the milk for about 30 seconds. Pour into the mug and serve hot.

This can also be served cold. Pour the dissolved matcha into a glass filled with ice. Leave the milk to cool slightly before frothing or whisking. Pour over ice and serve.

CITRUS GROVES

The introduction of the seedless navel orange in the late 1800s put California on the map making it the second largest citrus producer after Florida. Despite the transition of what was known as the Citrus Belt to the Central Valley, there are still hidden gems left in Southern California cultivating more than just navels. Located in Murrieta on 27 acres, Garcia Organic Farm grows over 33 varieties of citrus and maintains strict organic practices. From fingerlimes and mandarinquats to sweet limes and valentine pomelos, fruit from Juan and Coco Garcia is coveted by local chefs and purveyors nationwide. It could be the 30 years of experience or that all the fruit is hand picked by just two workers but head farmer and owner, Juan, credits the quality of the fruit to the simple notion of TLC.

ICED TEAS

Herbs and aromatics add another level to iced tea. With the Californian sun, some people steep their ingredients low and slow outside in a jar and enjoy the following day. If you prefer tea sweetened, try using kumquat syrup (see page 203).

makes 1.9 litres (64 fl oz)   **prep** 5 mins + at least 4 hours to steep & chill
cook 10 mins

LEMONGRASS & GINGER

3 lemongrass stalks, cut into thirds and lightly smashed

7.5 cm (3 in) piece of fresh ginger, sliced

Regular, Herb or Floral ice cubes (see page 215), to serve

Handful of basil or Thai basil, to serve

Place all the ingredients with 1.9 litres (64 fl oz) water in a large saucepan and bring to the boil. Reduce the heat and simmer for 10 minutes. Remove from the heat and leave the tea to cool to room temperature. Transfer to a large jar or bowl to steep for at least 4 hours, or overnight in the fridge. Strain before serving over ice with basil.

BLACK TEA & BLACKBERRY

290 g (10 oz) blackberries

4 black teabags of choice, tied together

Handful of mint, to serve

Regular, Herb or Floral ice cubes (see page 215), to serve

Slice half the blackberries and place in an extra-large jar. Add the teabags and 1.9 litres (64 fl oz) water and stir to combine and lightly mash the blackberries with a spoon. Place outside in the sun or on the work surface for at least 4 hours. Chill in the fridge overnight. The next day, remove the teabags and serve with the remaining berries and the mint over ice.

LEMON VERBENA

1 bunch of lemon verbena

Regular, Herb or Floral ice cubes (see page 215), to serve

2 lemons, sliced, to serve

Place the lemon verbena in a large heatproof bowl or pot. Pour 1.9 litres (64 fl oz) boiling water over the herbs. Cool and steep for at least 4 hours, or overnight in the fridge. Strain before serving over ice with lemon slices.

NUT MILK

Non-dairy milk options now are endless but the difference between a boxed version and freshly made are apparent. It's simple enough to make and a batch will last you through the week to use in your morning coffee or tea, granola and smoothie bowl.

---

150 g (5½ oz) raw brazil nuts or almonds or 140 g (5 oz) cashews or macadamia nuts

Pinch of sea salt flakes

makes 170 ml (5½ fl oz/⅔ cup)
prep overnight to soak   **cook** none

Place the nuts in a large container and cover with filtered water by 5 cm (2 in). Soak overnight.

The next day, strain, rinse and place in a blender. Add 710 ml (24 fl oz) filtered water and the salt and purée until smooth. Pour the mixture into a nut milk bag set over a large bowl. If you do not have a bag, triple line a fine sieve with muslin cloth. Squeeze the bag or push down on the pulp to extract as much milk as possible. Discard the solids (or save to dry out and use as a nut flour for baking). Store the milk in sealed containers in the fridge for up to 5 days.

Use for Golden Turmeric Latte (see page 47) or Nut Milk Panna Cotta (see page 191). Or sip cold or slightly warmed with a little sugar or honey to lightly sweeten.

Note: Also try with 140 g (5 oz) pumpkin or sunflower seeds.

CHERRY SHRUB

The local fruits are packed with so much flavour, it's no wonder eateries are making their own shrubs and tonics to make drinks. This way there is a happy union of sweet and tart with home-made soda. Shrub is also a great addition in cocktails.

450 g (1 lb) cherries, pitted, plus extra to garnish

5 sage sprigs

240 ml (8 fl oz) apple cider vinegar

220 g (8 oz) granulated or raw sugar

5 whole black peppercorns

Pinch of sea salt flakes

Regular, Herb or Floral ice cubes (see page 215), to serve

Sparkling water, to serve

makes 470 ml (16 fl oz)

prep 10 mins + 3–5 days to steep   **cook** 5 mins

Place the cherries and sage in a large jar.

Combine the vinegar, sugar, peppercorns and salt in a small saucepan and heat over medium–low heat for 2 minutes, whisking until the sugar has just dissolved.

Pour the vinegar mixture over the fruit and mash slightly with a wooden spoon. Leave to cool completely, then place the lid on the jar. Shake a few times to distribute the flavour. Chill in the fridge for 3–5 days to let the flavours infuse.

Strain and serve 3 tablespoons shrub over ice. Top up with sparkling water, stir and garnish with more cherries.

If using herb or floral ice cubes, there will be subtle hints of aromatics in the drink as the ice melts. Use other fruits and herbs throughout the season for variation. The strained shrub keeps for 1 month in the fridge.

LUNCH

There are no sad salads in California – even this most standard of lunch staples can be elevated with top-notch produce and unexpected elements. Midday meals for those living the office life often come from gourmet cafeterias, food trucks or neighbourhood eateries, but with their focus on sourcing seasonal and local products, even a typical lunch is far from basic. Quick and light is the way to go and simple dishes such as grain bowls, tacos and salads are transformed with bright, fresh ingredients.

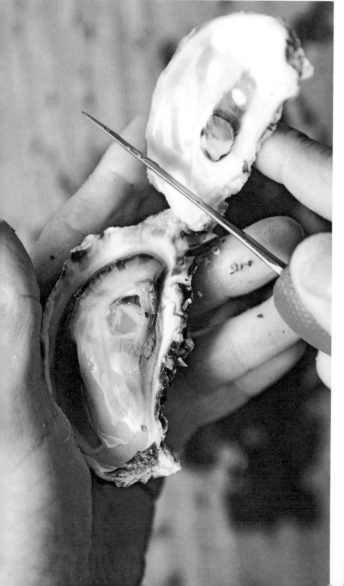

FISH SHACKS

The Pacific Coast Highway (PCH) hugs the entirety of California's coastline, making for one of the state's most scenic drives. Along its route you will find a number of fish shacks that serve distinctly different fare from north to south in the same way the trees change from fragrant eucalyptus to tall, swaying palms. Located in Marshall, just outside of San Francisco, Hog Island Oyster Company produces flavourful shellfish that are sustainably grown and harvested. Visitors can even shuck their own oysters in the picnic area while enjoying the serene surroundings. As the PCH winds further south the influence of Mexico is apparent in the perfectly fried fish tacos at the various roadside spots.

BAJA FISH TACOS

The best fried fish taco can sometimes be found in the most unexpected places, such as a stand located in a petrol station in San Diego. Inspired by the seafood-rich Baja region of Mexico, this dish simply requires a proper batter, a slaw and a good tortilla.

1 small red onion, finely sliced

Juice of 1 lime

Neutral oil, for frying

450 g (1 lb) skinless rock cod or similar white fish

250 g (9 oz/1⅔ cups) plain (all-purpose) flour

2 tablespoons baking powder

1 tablespoon cornflour (cornstarch)

1 large egg

350 ml (12 fl oz) dark Mexican beer

Sea salt flakes and freshly ground black pepper

12 small corn or flour tortillas (about 13 cm/5 in in diameter)

½ small green cabbage, finely sliced

8 radishes, sliced into matchsticks

2 tablespoons crema or sour cream

Fermented Hot Sauce (see page 213), optional

serves 4   **prep** 15 mins   **cook** 15 min

Place the onion in a small bowl. Pour the lime juice over and toss to combine. Stir occasionally while prepping other items.

Heat 7.5 cm (3 in) of oil in a large casserole dish or heavy saucepan to 190°C (375°F). Prepare a wire rack set over a baking sheet and set aside.

Pat the fish dry and divide into 13 cm (5 in) portions. Season.

Place 60 g (2 oz) of the flour on a plate and lightly coat the fish, shaking off any excess flour.

Combine the remaining flour, the baking powder, cornflour, egg, beer and 3 teaspoons salt in a large bowl and whisk well. Coat the fish letting any excess run off and carefully lower into the hot oil. Fry in 2–3 batches for 3–4 minutes, flipping once until deep golden. Adjust the heat to maintain the temperature. Place the fish on the prepared rack and lightly season with salt. Repeat with the remaining fish.

Meanwhile, toast the tortillas over a direct flame until lightly charred in spots, about 1 minute. Flip and repeat.

Place the cabbage, radishes and crema in a bowl and lightly toss to combine. Season.

Divide the fish among the tortillas, top with the cabbage mixture, reserved onions and hot sauce, if liked.

BLT

At the height of tomato season there's no better combination than these five simple ingredients.

---

12 thick-cut bacon slices, (about 510 g/1 lb 2 oz)

55 g (2 oz) mayonnaise

Sourdough loaf, 8 slices (about 1 cm/½ in thick)

1 small gem lettuce, leaves separated

2 large heirloom tomatoes, sliced

Sea salt flakes and freshly ground black pepper

serves 4   **prep** 5 mins   **cook** 35 mins

Arrange the bacon in a single layer in 2 separate large cast-iron frying pans. Place the pans over medium heat and cook for 10–12 minutes, flipping once halfway through, until the fat is rendered and the bacon is golden and crispy. Adjust the heat on the second side if the pan gets too hot and starts to smoke. Transfer the bacon to a plate lined with kitchen paper.

Discard the fat and wipe out the pans. Return the pans to medium heat. Spread a thin layer of mayonnaise on both sides of each slice of bread and toast in the pans, in batches, for 5 minutes, or until golden, and flip. Repeat with the remaining slices.

To assemble the sandwiches, spread the remaining mayonnaise on all the toasted bread. Top 4 slices with bacon, lettuce and tomato slices. Season lightly and close with the remaining bread. Cut in half. Serve.

SUMMER SALAD

The California summers flood the farmers' markets with ingredients that are so tasty in their raw form, sometimes a dinner can be thrown together with minimal cooking. This salad is all about the various textures and flavours complementing each other.

---

80 ml (2½ fl oz/⅓ cup) extra virgin olive oil

2 tablespoons amaranth

680 g (1½ lb) mixed colour and size heirloom tomatoes

115 g (4 oz) small summer squash mix

115 g (4 oz) small lemon cucumbers (or other summer variety)

3 tablespoons pickling liquid (see page 209)

Sea salt flakes and freshly ground black pepper

2 corn-on-the-cobs, husked and kernels removed

1 shallot, finely sliced

6 basil sprigs, leaves picked

serves 4   **prep** 5 mins   **cook** 5 min

Heat a medium saucepan over medium heat. Add 1 tablespoon of the olive oil and all the amaranth and cover. Shake occasionally until the grains are toasted and have popped, about 1 minute. Transfer to a bowl and set aside.

Slice the large tomatoes crossways and halve or quarter the smaller tomatoes. Finely slice the squash and cucumbers. Use a mandolin if it is easier.

Whisk the pickling liquid and the remaining olive oil in a small bowl. Season.

Arrange the tomatoes, squash and cucumbers on a large platter. Season lightly. Top with the corn, shallot and season again. Drizzle the dressing over everything and top with basil leaves and the popped amaranth.

CAULIFLOWER RICE BOWL

Vegetables chopped small to resemble rice has become a wildly popular alternative for those who have a grain-free lifestyle. Cauliflower has a sturdy texture that mimics a kernel of rice. With the flavour being neutral, it is a great base to eat with anything.

1 small cauliflower (about 1 kg/2 lb 3 oz), cut into florets

115 g (4 oz) home-made Pesto (see page 207)

Sea salt flakes and freshly ground black pepper

225 g (8 oz) smoked fish, such as trout, mackerel or sardines, flaked

4 celery stalks, finely sliced, plus inner leaves to garnish

115 g (4 oz) pitted green olives, chopped

40 g (1½ oz) Marcona almonds, roughly chopped

Small handful of small basil leaves, torn

1 small lemon, cut into wedges, to serve

serves 4　**prep** 10 mins　**cook** none

Pulse the cauliflower in a food processor for about 1 minute until it is chopped to about the size of rice, scraping down the side once halfway through. Transfer to a bowl and stir in half the pesto until evenly coated. Season to taste. Top with the smoked fish, celery, celery leaves, olives, almonds, basil and the remaining pesto. Serve with lemon wedges.

VEGETABLE DUMPLINGS SOUP

A fresher, lighter take on Chinese wontons, these spring-filled parcels are simple to make once you get the hang of it. They are also great to freeze if you want to make them ahead of time.

140 g (5 oz) shelled garden peas (about 450 g/1 lb whole pods)

140 g (5 oz) shelled broad (fava) beans (about 450 g/1 lb whole beans)

1 bunch of snow peas (mangetout) or broad (fava) bean leaves (about 125 g/4½ oz leaves)

115 g (4 oz) silken tofu

4 spring (green) onions, finely sliced

10 basil leaves

1 teaspoon sea salt

½ teaspoon ground white pepper

32 square wonton wrappers

1.15 litres (39 fl oz) vegetable stock or bone broth (see page 197 or 199)

serves 4   **prep** 40 mins   **cook** 15 mins

Bring a small saucepan of salted water to the boil. Prepare an ice bath. Add the peas and blanch for 1 minute, or until bright green. Use a slotted spoon to transfer the peas to the ice bath, then when cool, use a slotted spoon to remove and set aside. Save the blanching water and ice bath and repeat with the broad beans. Once the broad beans are cool, slip the skins off and discard.

Place three-quarters of the leaves, the tofu, 3 spring onions, the basil, 1 teaspoon salt and ½ teaspoon pepper in a food processor and process for 1 minute to combine, stopping once to scrape down the side. Add three-quarters of the peas and broad beans and set the rest aside to garnish. Pulse 2–3 times until just combined but still chunky.

Working in batches, lay a few wrappers on a work surface. Keep the remaining covered with a dish towel to prevent them drying out. Place about 2 teaspoons of the filling in the centre of each wrapper. Lightly dampen the edges with water and fold into a rectangle, pushing out any air. Press to seal. Wet one corner on the long end and join the other to seal. Repeat with the remaining dumplings.

Bring the stock to the boil in a medium saucepan. Turn to the lowest setting and cover to keep hot. Add the reserved peas and broad beans. Season.

Bring a large saucepan of salted water to the boil. Lower in half the dumplings and simmer for 5 minutes, or until they float to the top. Use a sieve to gently remove and divide between 2 bowls. Repeat with the remaining dumplings. Ladle the hot stock with the peas and beans over the dumplings and top with the reserved spring onions and leaves. Season lightly.

GRILLED MEATBALLS WITH LETTUCE WRAPS

There is a whole world beyond just pho in Vietnamese cuisine. This Vietnamese-style dish mirrors the freshness of Californian cuisine with grilled meat wrapped in fragrant herbs and lettuce to form a harmonious bite.

450 g (1 lb) minced (ground) pork, not lean

1 tablespoon fish sauce

2 tablespoons maple syrup

1 small shallot, finely chopped

1 teaspoon ground black pepper

½ teaspoon sea salt

Rapeseed or neutral olive oil, for brushing

Dipping sauce:

2 tablespoons fish sauce

2 tablespoons lime juice

2 teaspoons granulated sugar

1 garlic clove, grated

1–2 Thai chillies, finely chopped

Finely sliced cucumber, radish, green mango or green papaya, for sauce

Accompaniments:

115 g (4 oz) rice noodles

2 small gem lettuces or mild mustard green leaves, to serve

Mixed herbs, such as Thai basil, shiso, perilla, dill, mint, to serve

serves 4 **prep** 10 mins
cook 10 mins + 10 mins soaking time for noodles

Combine the pork, fish sauce, maple syrup, shallot, pepper and salt in a large bowl and mix gently with your hands until just combined. Divide into 20 balls, about 1 slightly rounded tablespoon, and lightly flatten. Set aside.

Bring a saucepan of water to the boil. Submerge the noodles, remove from the heat and soak for 10 minutes. Drain and rinse in cold water.

Heat a griller (broiler) to medium high.

For the sauce, combine the fish sauce, lime juice, sugar and garlic in a bowl and whisk until the sugar has dissolved. Stir in 125 ml (4 fl oz/½ cup) water and desired amount of chillies, then add the sliced vegetables and fruit.

Lightly brush the tops of the meatballs with oil, then place, oiled side down, on the griller rack and grill (broil) for 3–4 minutes until nicely charred in spots. Flip and cook for another 3–4 minutes until just cooked through.

Serve the meatballs with the dipping sauce, noodles, greens and herbs. Wrap and enjoy.

SEAWEED HARVEST

The rocky coastline and cold waters of Northern California create an ideal environment for seaweed to thrive. Low tide exposes the abundant edible algae that Heidi Herrmann of Strong Arm Farm wild harvests. Heidi speaks of the seaweed that grows off the Sonoma County coast with infectious excitement, leaving chefs, customers and foraging class students with a deeper appreciation for this easily overlooked food. Rehydrate dried seaweed by soaking it in a large bowl of water for use in soups or salads, or crumble toasted nori on top of grain bowls or eggs.

PACIFIC COAST SOUP

The crisp ocean air in Northern California inspired this soup. When making a dashi (Japanese soup base), start with kombu and various other dried ingredients that impart an umami flavour. It leaves a clean, clear broth as a base to build upon.

2 pieces kombu (about 15 x 8 cm/6 x 3¼ in)

10 dried shiitake mushrooms

1 tablespoon soy sauce

2 teaspoons sea salt flakes

30 g (1 oz) mixed dried seaweed, such as bladder wrack, arame and dulse

480 g (1 lb 1 oz) silken tofu, cut into 4 pieces

225 g (8 oz) lump crabmeat

Cooked white or brown rice, to serve

Handful of Japanese or regular parsley leaves, to serve

3 spring (green) onions, finely sliced, to serve

serves 4   **prep** 10 mins   **cook** 1 hour 5 mins

Place the kombu and mushrooms in a large saucepan or casserole dish and add 2.8 litres (95 fl oz) water. Leave for 20 minutes to hydrate the kombu and mushrooms, then bring to a very gentle simmer and cook for 1 hour, or until it is reduced by about a quarter. Remove the kombu and mushrooms. Stir in the soy sauce and salt.

Discard the kombu and finely slice the mushrooms. Return the sliced mushrooms to the pan and add the mixed seaweed, tofu and crab. Simmer gently until just heated through. Place a little cooked rice in each bowl. Divide the soup among the bowls and top with a handful of herbs and spring onions.

SUNSHINE BOWL

The sunshine bowl is influenced from Chinese congee. There are Californian restaurants that serve their own take on this comforting dish, incorporating traditional as well as unexpected ingredients.

450 g (1 lb) flaky white fish, such as red snapper or striped bass, skin removed and reserved, meat sliced into 2.5 cm (1 in) pieces

Sea salt flakes and ground white pepper

390 g (14 oz) cooked long-grain white rice, cold

2.5 cm (1 in) piece of fresh ginger, peeled and slightly smashed

4 large eggs

1 tablespoon rapeseed or other neutral oil

2 spring (green) onions, finely sliced

4 inner celery stalks and leaves, chopped

70 g (2½ oz) toasted pine nuts

serves 4   **prep** 10 mins   **cook** 45 mins

Season the fish and skin with salt and set aside.

Place the rice in a saucepan with 1.9 litres (64 fl oz) water, the ginger and 2 teaspoons salt and bring to a gentle boil. Cover partially with a lid and gently simmer for 45 minutes, stirring to the bottom occasionally until the rice breaks down and has a creamy texture. Add a little more water if the consistency is too thick.

Meanwhile, bring a small saucepan of water to the boil. Use enough water to cover 4 eggs by 2.5 cm (1 in). Lower the eggs into the water and simmer for 7 minutes. Transfer the eggs to an ice bath. Gently crack the eggs all around and leave to cool just enough to handle. Peel, slice in half and reserve.

Add the oil to a cold frying pan. Pat the fish skins dry, lay down flat and weigh with another pan to ensure even contact. Cook over medium heat for 5–6 minutes until the skin is golden brown and crispy. Remove the weight, flip and cook for another 3–4 minutes until completely crisp. Transfer to a plate lined with kitchen paper and sprinkle with a little salt.

When the porridge is ready, add the fish pieces and cook for 2–3 minutes until heated through. Ladle the porridge into 4 bowls. Add the egg, spring onions, celery, pine nuts and fish skin. Season and serve.

Note: This recipe is a great use of leftover rice. If you don't have leftover rice, cook 190 g (6½ oz) dry. Rinse and drain the rice 10 times, or until the water is mainly clear. Drain and transfer to a rice cooker or saucepan and add 240 ml (8 fl oz) water. Cook according to the rice cooker's manual. If using a pan, bring to the boil, then cover, reduce the heat to medium–low and simmer for 10–12 minutes until tender and the water is absorbed. Remove from the heat, cover and leave for 5 minutes. Transfer to a baking sheet or dish and cool in the freezer for 20 minutes before using.

SKILLET VEGETABLE BOWL

There is a little of every flavour spectrum in this dish, fermented umami from the miso, sweetness from the vegetables and herbs, nuttiness from the rice, creaminess from the avocado and a sprinkling of salt from the seasoning.

---

190 g (6½ oz) brown rice, rinsed well and drained

75 g (2¾ oz) white mild miso

1 tablespoon soy sauce

1 garlic clove, grated

2 tablespoons extra virgin olive oil

225 g (8 oz) small mixed colour carrots, scrubbed

225 g (8 oz) small Japanese turnips, scrubbed and halved

225 g (8 oz) small radishes, scrubbed

2 small avocados, halved

½ bunch of Japanese or regular parsley, leaves picked

Gomasio or furikake seasoning

serves 4　**prep** 10 mins　**cook** 35 mins

Rinse the rice in a small saucepan a few times until the water runs clear. Drain and return the rice to the pan with 360 ml (12 fl oz) water. Bring to the boil. Cover and reduce the heat to medium–low and simmer for 35 minutes, or until the rice is tender and the water is absorbed. Remove from the heat and leave for 5 minutes. Alternatively, cook in a rice cooker according to the instruction manual.

Meanwhile, whisk the miso, 60 ml (2 fl oz/¼ cup) water, soy sauce and garlic together in a small bowl until combined. Set aside.

Heat a large cast-iron frying pan over medium–high heat. Add the olive oil and the vegetables and cook for 5–8 minutes, stirring occasionally to get an even colour. Add the miso mixture, reduce the heat to medium and cook for 10 minutes, stirring occasionally to ensure the vegetables are evenly coated and crisp tender.

Serve the vegetables with the rice, avocado, parsley and a generous sprinkling of seasoning mix.

CALIFORNIA TUNA BOWL

The fresh seafood and greens available make it easy to recreate this Californian version of the Hawaiian poke bowl. For different seasonal variations, opt for shellfish and other vegetables with a crunch.

190 g (6½ oz) quinoa

2 tablespoons toasted sesame oil

2 tablespoons extra virgin olive oil

1 tablespoon soy sauce

Grated zest and juice of 2 lemons

450 g (1 lb) sushi-grade tuna, diced

280 g (10 oz) chopped crunchy greens such as sugar snap peas, broccolini, asparagus

100 g (3½ oz) small leafy greens such as rocket (arugula), pea shoots, spinach

1 short cucumber, finely sliced

6 radishes, finely sliced

140 g (5 oz) pickled carrots, sliced (see page 209)

40 g (1½ oz) pumpkin seeds, toasted

Sea salt flakes and freshly ground black pepper

2 tablespoons sesame seeds, toasted, to serve

serves 4   **prep** 15 mins +10 mins cooling
cook 20 mins

Toast the quinoa in a small saucepan for 3–5 minutes until fragrant, stirring a few times. Add 350 ml (12 fl oz) water and bring to a simmer. Cover and reduce the heat to medium–low and cook for 13–15 minutes until all the water is absorbed. Remove from the heat and keep covered for another 5 minutes. Fluff and leave to cool for 10 minutes.

Place the sesame and olive oils, soy sauce, lemon zest and juice, ½ teaspoon salt and ½ teaspoon pepper in a small bowl and whisk to combine.

Divide the quinoa, tuna, crunchy and leafy greens, cucumber, radishes, pickles and pumpkin seeds among 4 bowls. Season lightly and serve with the dressing and sesame seeds.

SPRING PRAWN SALAD

Springtime brings with it a lot of delicate flavours and textures, which makes this salad pair well with the sweetness of the Santa Barbara ridgeback prawns. Substitute with any local, wild, smaller, sweet prawns.

1 bunch of asparagus

3 spring (green) onions

3 fresh bay leaves

8 whole black peppercorns

450 g (1 lb) raw Santa Barbara ridgeback prawns (shrimp) or local small prawns, peeled and deveined

125 ml (4 fl oz/½ cup) thinned Avocado Green Goddess (see page 211)

180 g (6½ oz) sugar snap peas or snow peas (mangetout), halved lengthways on a bias

1 bunch of pea shoot leaves, tough stems removed

Sea salt flakes and freshly ground black pepper

60 g (2 oz) pistachios, roughly chopped

serves 4   **prep** 5 mins   **cook** 10 mins

Bring a saucepan of salted water to the boil. Prepare an ice bath. Add the asparagus and cook for 1 minute until just bright. Remove and transfer to the ice bath. Once cool, drain the asparagus in a colander.

Place the spring onions, bay leaves and whole peppercorns in the pan and return to the boil. Add the prawns, cover and turn off the heat. Poach for 8–10 minutes until just cooked through. Strain and discard the aromatics, then toss the prawns with 2 tablespoons of the Avocado Green Goddess dressing and leave to cool.

Place the sugar snap peas and pea shoot leaves in a large bowl. Add half the remaining dressing, season and toss lightly.

Season the asparagus and serve with the prawns, topped with the sugar snap peas and leaves. Sprinkle the pistachios on top and serve with the remaining dressing.

THE VW VAN

Symbolic of the surf community and California's laid-back vibe, the vintage Volkswagen bus is a cherished relic, especially the many models that perfectly suit the nomadic lifestyle of surfers in search of the best waves. A pop-top ensures a more spacious sleeping area for comfortable beachside nights while the kitchenette allows for home-cooked meals even while on the road. In fact, it's the perfect set-up for making a morning green shake or enjoying a surfer's breakfast after a sunrise session.

HOLLYWOOD SALAD

This salad is derived from the Cobb, which originated in a Hollywood restaurant. Rather than add bacon, the use of the fried chicken skin resembles that same delightful saltiness and crunch and nothing goes to waste.

3 whole chicken thighs (about 450 g/1 lb) total, skins separated

Sea salt flakes and freshly ground black pepper

60 ml (2 fl oz/¼ cup) extra virgin olive oil

2 large eggs

3 tablespoons rice wine vinegar

1 bunch of chives and flowers (if available), chopped

3 small gem lettuces, leaves separated

250 g (9 oz) mixed cherry tomatoes, halved if large

1 avocado, sliced

55 g (2 oz) blue cheese, sliced

serves 4   **prep** 10 mins   **cook** 40 mins

Preheat the oven to 190°C (375°F).

Dry the chicken and skins well. Season all over with salt and pepper. Add 1 tablespoon of the olive oil to a cold cast-iron frying pan. Lay the chicken skins down flat and weigh with another pan to ensure even contact. Cook over medium heat for 5–6 minutes until the skin is golden brown and crispy. Remove the weight, flip and cook for another 3–4 minutes until completely crisp. Transfer to a plate lined with kitchen paper and set aside. Add the chicken thighs, bone side down, and place the pan in the oven. Roast for 15–20 minutes until the chicken is just cooked through. Cool slightly and shred the chicken.

Meanwhile, bring a small saucepan of water to the boil. Lower the eggs into the water and simmer for 10 minutes. Transfer the eggs to an ice bath. Gently crack the eggs all around and leave to cool just enough to handle. Peel and grate the eggs on a box grater.

Whisk the remaining olive oil, the vinegar and half the chives together in a small bowl. Season.

Place the lettuce in a large bowl. Drizzle over half the dressing and toss gently. Arrange on individual plates or a large platter. Top with the shredded chicken, tomatoes, avocado, cheese and grated egg. Drizzle over another spoonful of the dressing. Crumble the reserved chicken skins on top of the salad and finish with the remaining chives and flowers, if using. Serve with the remaining dressing, if liked.

SHAVED BRASSICA SALAD

So often brassicas are roasted or grilled. When in season and young, this hearty winter salad is great raw. Although finely shaved, these greens are sturdy enough to withstand the robust dressing.

3 tablespoons pine nuts

1½ teaspoons sesame seeds

1½ teaspoons coriander seeds

1½ teaspoons cumin seeds

1 small romanesco broccoli

255 g (8 oz) brussels sprouts, shaved

1 bunch of broccolini, cut into 2.5 cm (1 in) pieces

90 g (3 oz) pitted green olives

Grated zest and juice of 1 lemon

3 marjoram sprigs, leaves picked

3 anchovy fillets

1 teaspoon chilli flakes

125 ml (4 fl oz/½ cup) extra virgin olive oil

½ preserved lemon, rinsed, rind chopped (see page 217)

Sea salt flakes and freshly ground black pepper

Parmesan, shaved, to serve

serves 4 **prep** 10 mins **cook** 10 mins

Toast the pine nuts in a small frying pan over medium–low heat for 5 minutes until fragrant. Add the sesame, coriander and cumin seeds and toast for another 3 minutes, or until the pine nuts are golden. Remove from the pan to cool, then roughly chop or smash with a mortar and pestle. Set aside.

Quarter the romanesco and finely slice crossways with a mandolin. Place the romanesco, brussels sprouts and broccolini in a large bowl and set aside.

Place the olives, lemon zest and juice, marjoram, anchovies and chilli flakes in a food processor. With the motor running, add the olive oil and process until a smooth dressing forms, scraping down the side once if necessary. Add the dressing to the vegetables, then add the preserved lemon and toss thoroughly, massaging the vegetables to soften slightly. Season lightly.

Divide the salad among 4 shallow bowls. Top with shaved parmesan and a sprinkle of the pine nut spice mixture.

SPRING GREENS SOUP

A simple pea and mint soup can rejuvenate you the way the arrival of spring brings a freshness to the air. This soup can be enjoyed at any temperature – soothing when warm and refreshing when cold.

1.8 kg (4 lb) whole garden peas, pods set aside

2 small leeks (230 g/8 oz), white and light green parts chopped

½ bunch (40 g/1½ oz) of mint, leaves picked from half

Sea salt flakes and ground white pepper

40 g (1½ oz) hemp seeds, to serve

Toppings:

125 g (4½ oz) raw or blanched chopped spring greens, peas and flowers

serves 4   **prep** 20 mins   **cook** 1 hour 5 mins

Place the pea pods, leeks, 1.9 litres (64 fl oz) water and 2 teaspoons sea salt in a large saucepan. Bring to the boil, stirring occasionally to help the pods meld, then reduce the heat to medium and cook for 1 hour, or until reduced by half. Turn off the heat and stir in the mint sprigs and steep for 5 minutes. Strain the stock and set aside. Wipe out the pan and return 710 ml (24 fl oz) stock to the boil. Reserve the remaining stock. Add the shelled peas and cook for 3 minutes, or until bright and just tender. Add the remaining mint leaves, then use a stick blender to purée until smooth or carefully transfer to a blender. Season with salt and pepper.

Serve hot or cold with spring greens, peas and flowers of choice and a sprinkling of hemp seeds. If serving cold, use the reserved stock to thin, if needed.

Note: When peas are not in season, this can be made with frozen peas. For additional flavour, make the stock with more aromatics (leeks, bay, thyme and spring/green onions) to replace the pods or use the vegetable stock on page 197.

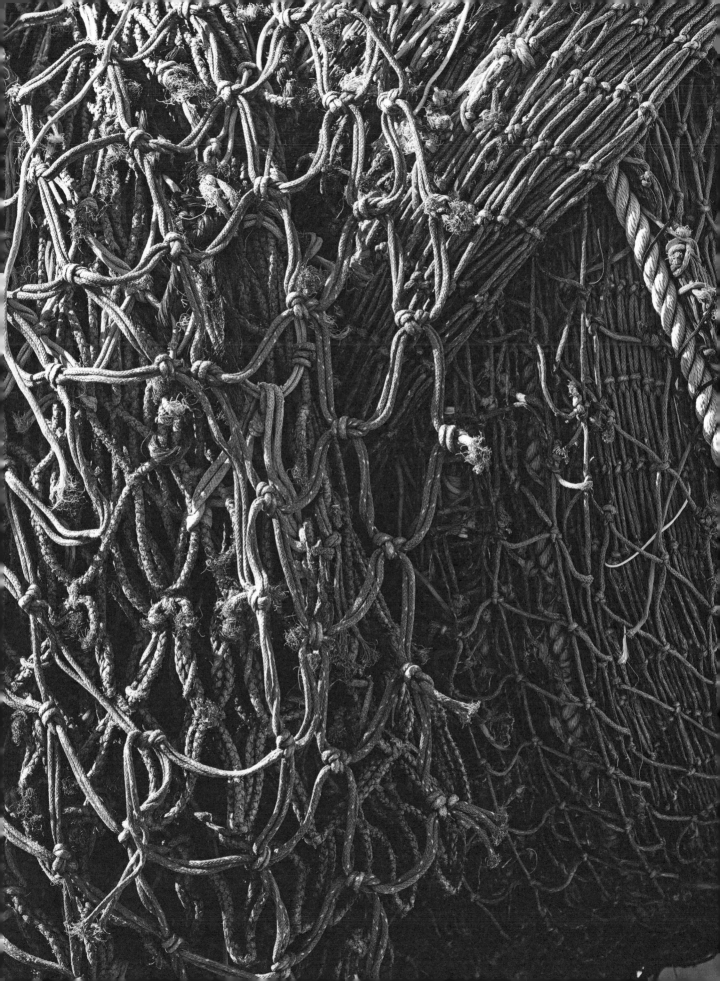

CRUNCHY WRAPS

Other cultures' version of a wrap may involve pittas, flatbreads, tortillas or lavash. A Californian spin-off typically showcases more greens and market vegetables. Wraps are a convenient meal for lunch since they are packaged so nicely to go.

---

190 g (6½ oz) short-grain brown rice

8 large spring greens or large green cabbage leaves (about 250 g/9 oz)

240 g (8½ oz) pickled beets (and shallots), sliced, plus 1 tablespoon brine (see page 209)

2 tablespoons extra virgin olive oil

2 avocados, stoned

2 tablespoons tahini

½ roasted chicken, meat shredded (about 250 g/9 oz)

24 basil leaves

80 g (2¾ oz) mixed sprouts

Sea salt flakes and freshly ground black pepper

serves 4   **prep** 10 mins   **cook** 35 mins

Rinse the rice in a large saucepan a few times until the water runs clear. Drain and return the rice to the pan with 360 ml (12 fl oz) water. Bring to the boil. Cover and reduce the heat to medium–low and simmer for 35 minutes, or until tender and the water is absorbed. Remove from the heat and leave for 5 minutes. Alternatively, cook in a rice cooker according to the instruction manual.

Meanwhile, prepare the spring greens. Lay a leaf, rib side up, and carefully shave off the rounded part of the rib with a paring knife held parallel to the chopping board. This will make it easier to wrap. Continue with the remaining leaves. Prepare an ice bath in a large bowl. Bring a large saucepan of salted water to the boil and blanch the spring greens for 10 seconds, or until pliable and bright green, then transfer to the ice bath to cool. Drain and lay on kitchen paper. Pat dry.

Place the pickle brine, 1 tablespoon of the olive oil, ½ teaspoon salt and ½ teaspoon pepper in a small bowl and whisk to combine. Pour over the rice and fluff with a fork.

Scoop out the avocado and place in a bowl. Add the tahini and ½ teaspoon salt and mash with a fork until combined. Add the remaining olive oil to loosen if the tahini is very firm.

Lay a spring green leaf with the long side towards you, shaved rib up. Spread an eighth of the avocado mix in the centre, leaving 5 cm (2 in) on the right and left sides. Layer an eighth each of the remaining ingredients: rice, sliced beet, chicken, basil and sprouts, and season. Roll the long end over once. Fold the right and left sides in and continue rolling the long side over. Continue with the remaining spring greens and ingredients. Serve 2 wraps per person.

SMALL BITES

Lighter fare is well suited to the Californian lifestyle – with plenty of al fresco dinners, beach trips and canyon hikes on the agenda a go-to repertoire of smaller, shareable bites is a must. These recipes, from yellowtail aguachile to lemony burrata flatbread, will be the stars of any outdoor spread, whether it is a picnic for two under the stars, a garden soirée or a neighbourhood gathering at a local park.

FARMERS' MARKETS

The farmers' markets in California are awe-inspiring. The vast array of produce on display every week makes you appreciate the magic of the state's fertile land. During the spring, every new crop of greens has flavourful edible flowers sprouting. Young broad (fava) beans are so tender they can be eaten whole, outer pods and all. At the peak of summer the market explodes with endless varieties of melons, stone fruit, raspberries and colourful shelling beans that look like mini jewels. Fresh ginger and mustard greens arrive in the autumn, while citrus and squash fill the markets in winter.

CALIFORNIA BARS

The ingredients in this bar will provide energy for your day. Customise this list of nuts and dried fruit to your liking. Cut and wrap into individual squares for easy transport.

10 Medjool dates, pitted

150 g (5½ oz) almonds, roughly chopped

120 g (4½ oz) rolled oats

80 g (2¾ oz) hemp seeds

60 g (2 oz) golden linseeds (flax seeds)

3 tablespoons sesame seeds

110 g (4 oz) coconut oil

80 ml (2½ fl oz) maple syrup

300 g (10½ oz) mixed dried fruit, such as strawberries, persimmons and sultanas (golden raisins), roughly chopped if large

1 teaspoon sea salt flakes

serves 6–8   **prep** 15 mins   **cook** 20 mins

Preheat the oven to 180°C (350°F).

Place the dates in a small heatproof bowl and cover with hot water. Leave to soften for 10 minutes.

Line a 20 cm (8 in) square baking tin with greaseproof paper with an overhang on the sides and set aside.

Combine the almonds, oats, hemp seeds, linseeds and sesame seeds on a baking sheet and toast for 20 minutes, or until lightly golden brown, turning once halfway through. Remove and leave to cool.

Meanwhile, place the coconut oil and maple syrup in a small saucepan over medium–low heat and whisk until just melted and combined. Cool slightly, then transfer to a high-speed blender. Drain the dates well, add to the blender and purée until very smooth, then transfer to a large bowl.

Add the toasted granola mixture, fruit and salt and toss well to combine. Press the mixture evenly into the prepared baking tin and leave to cool completely. Remove from the tin and cut into bars. Store in an airtight container for up to a week.

CITRUS SALAD

The anticipation for the beautiful Californian citrus builds when the fragrant blossoms appear in the months leading up to fruiting season, when the state erupts with an abundance of citrus. This recipe transforms the fruit into a salad of many flavours.

1 small pomelo

1 pink grapefruit

2 navel, cara cara or blood oranges

1 celery stalk, plus inner leaves

Extra virgin olive oil, for drizzling

2 mandarins, peeled and sliced crossways

8 kumquats, finely sliced crossways

60 g (2 oz) pistachios, shelled and chopped

Sea salt flakes

serves 4   **prep** 15 mins   **cook** none

Peel the thick skin off the pomelo, then remove enough of the outer white pith to be able to separate the pomelo into individual segments. Run a small paring knife along the flat side of a segment to release the inner fruit from the membrane. Repeat with the remaining segments.

Slice the top and bottom off the grapefruit to expose the fruit. Use a paring knife to remove the skin and pith following the curve of the fruit. Slice crossways to make rounds. Reserve the accumulated juices in a bowl and set aside. Repeat with the oranges.

Shave the celery with a peeler or mandolin. Cut the ribbons down into bite-sized pieces. Place the celery and leaves in the bowl with the reserved juices. Drizzle with a little olive oil and lightly toss.

To serve, arrange all the mixed citrus on a platter or individual plates. Top with the dressed celery, pistachios and a light sprinkling of salt.

TACOS

Taco trucks and stands are a dime a dozen in California, but that doesn't make the tasty fare they serve any less priceless. Each one has a distinct speciality, and locals will happily wait in long lines day and night for their favourite al pastor taco, crispy hard-shelled or seafood tostada. Most spots serve a range of grilled meat including carne asada, carnitas, lengua, cabeza, tripa and buche. The typical street taco is made up of two soft corn tortillas topped with a mound of meat that customers can garnish with their favourite salsa bar fixings: hot sauce, lime, jalapeños, onions, coriander (cilantro) and radishes.

SUMMER GUACAMOLE & CHIPS

Guacamole is an easy dish to prepare in minutes and can be eaten with just about anything – chips, crackers, bread, crudités. This version includes pops of sweetness with raw summer corn and a crunch from the pumpkin seeds.

Juice of 1 lime

1 garlic clove, grated

2 avocados, stoned and diced

1 corn-on-the-cob, husked and kernels removed

125 g (4½ oz) cherry tomatoes, halved or quartered if large

2 spring (green) onions, finely chopped

40 g (1½ oz) toasted pumpkin seeds

1 small jalapeño chilli, finely sliced

Sea salt flakes and freshly ground black pepper

Tortilla chips, to serve

serves 4   **prep** 5 mins   **cook** none

Add the lime juice and garlic to a bowl and stir to combine. Add the avocados, corn, tomatoes and half each of the spring onions, pumpkin seeds and jalapeño. Season with salt and pepper and mix gently to combine. Garnish with the remaining spring onions, pumpkin seeds and jalapeño to serve. Enjoy with tortilla chips.

AGUACHILE

There is a well-known seafood taco truck in Los Angeles that serves aguachile as well as a dish that comes with a high spice level warning. Aguachile translates to chilli water so adjust the chilli type in this recipe according to your desired heat level.

1 green tomato (280 g/10 oz), chopped

2 short cucumbers, very finely sliced

2 shallots, very finely sliced

½ habanero chilli, seeded

1 tablespoon grated ginger

60 ml (2 fl oz/¼ cup) lime juice

Sea salt flakes and freshly ground black pepper

10 mixed small radishes, very finely sliced

340 g (12 oz) sushi-grade skinless fish, such as yellowtail, halibut or snapper, medium dice

Extra virgin olive oil, for drizzling

Coriander (cilantro) leaves or flowers, to garnish

Charred corn tortillas or saltines, to serve

serves 4–6   **prep** 10 mins   **cook** none

Place the tomato, half the cucumbers, half the shallots, the habanero, ginger and lime juice in a blender and purée for 1 minute, or until very smooth. Season with salt and pepper.

Arrange the radishes, the remaining cucumbers and the fish on a platter. Season lightly. Spoon the aguachile over the fish and vegetables. Top with the remaining shallots and a drizzle of olive oil. Garnish with coriander and serve with tortillas or saltines, if liked.

LEMONY BURRATA FLATBREAD

Middle Eastern flavours have a well-established place in Californian cuisine. The zippy spice combinations and ingredients are an accent to the mild creamy cheese here.

---

280 g (10 oz) burrata, torn into pieces

4 pieces flatbread, toasted

½ preserved lemon, rinsed, rind finely sliced (see page 217)

4 Medjool dates, pitted and finely sliced

60 g (2 oz) pistachios, chopped

Small handful of wood sorrel

½ teaspoon za'atar

Sea salt flakes and freshly ground black pepper

Honey, to serve

serves 4   **prep** 5 mins   **cook** none

Divide the burrata among the bread. Top with the preserved lemon, dates, pistachios and sorrel. Sprinkle with za'atar and season lightly. Serve with a drizzle of honey.

BROAD BEAN HUMMUS

A loose play on traditional hummus, this can be made with many other market ingredients, such as white beans and cashews, beets and tahini.

1.6 kg (3½ lb) whole broad (fava) beans in pods

Grated zest and juice of 1 lemon

40 g (1½ oz) pumpkin seeds

1 spring (green) onion, sliced, white and green parts, separated

4 tablespoons extra virgin olive oil

Sea salt flakes

Crackers and/or crudités, to serve

serves 4–6   **makes** 450 g (1 lb)   **prep** 25 mins
cook 5 mins

Bring a small saucepan of salted water to the boil. Prepare an ice bath. Add the beans and blanch for 1–2 minutes until the shells have just loosened. Use a slotted spoon to transfer the beans to the ice bath. When cooled, slip the shells off and discard.

In a food processor, combine the beans, lemon zest, 1 tablespoon juice, 1 tablespoon water, ½ teaspoon salt, 2 tablespoons pumpkin seeds, the white part of the spring onions and 2 tablespoons of the olive oil and process until smooth, scraping down the side as necessary. Add 1 more teaspoon water at a time if needed to achieve desired consistency. Transfer to a bowl to serve.

Heat the remaining olive oil in a small saucepan until just hot. Carefully add the remaining pumpkin seeds, the spring onion greens and swirl. Leave to cool slightly, then drizzle over the hummus. Season lightly and serve with crackers and/or crudités.

CALIFORNIA HAND ROLLS

Rather than rolling into a cone, this hand roll is shaped like a cylinder so each bite has equal filling. When in season, Dungeness crab would be ideal but any sweet lump crabmeat from your fishmonger will do.

---

190 g (6½ oz) sushi rice

1 tablespoon rice wine vinegar

1 tablespoon granulated sugar

1½ teaspoons sea salt

6 large sheets roasted seaweed (from 30 g/1 oz pack)

340 g (12 oz) cooked crabmeat

2 small Japanese cucumbers, halved crossways and sliced into matchsticks

1 avocado, stoned and sliced into 12 thin wedges

40 g (1½ oz) sprouts of choice

Toasted sesame seeds, to garnish

Soy sauce, to serve

Wasabi, to serve

Lemon wedges, to serve

serves 4   **prep** 15 mins   **cook** 15 mins

Rinse and drain the rice 10 times, or until the water runs clear. Drain well and transfer to a rice cooker or small saucepan and add 240 ml (8 fl oz) water. Cook according to the rice cooker's manual. If using a pan, bring to the boil over medium–high heat, cover, reduce the heat to medium–low and cook for 10 minutes, or until tender and the water is absorbed. Remove from the heat and leave, covered, for 5 minutes. Transfer to a large shallow bowl.

Meanwhile, heat the vinegar, sugar and salt in a small saucepan over medium–low heat for 1–2 minutes, stirring until just dissolved. Sprinkle over the rice and fluff with a rice paddle or a wooden spoon. Cool slightly before using.

Cut the seaweed sheets in half crossways and lay the short side towards you. Working quickly with damp hands, gently press a thin layer of rice to cover two-thirds of the sheet leaving the opposite end empty. In the middle of the rice, arrange a heaped tablespoon of crab into a line the width of the seaweed, 5 cucumber sticks, a slice of avocado and a small amount of sprouts to just cover. Lightly sprinkle with sesame seeds. Roll away from you and end seam side down. Enjoy immediately or very lightly dab the edge of the seaweed to seal. Repeat with the remaining ingredients. Serve with soy sauce, wasabi and lemon.

Note: Roasted seaweed sheets typically come in large rectangles, (about 21 x 19.5 cm/8¼ x 7¾ in) sheets. To add a little crisp to the seaweed, wave once or twice quickly over a flame.

VINEYARDS

Paso Robles, Mendocino and the Santa Cruz Mountains are just a few of the notable wine areas in California but none are more celebrated than Napa and Sonoma. Picturesque and bursting with great food it is easy to spend a weekend in wine country marvelling at the surroundings, especially when the Mariani sibling-run vineyard in Sonoma is on the list. Everything at Scribe Winery – the hacienda, the food, the wine, the dishware – is a tribute to the land, and embodies the laissez-faire attitude that makes California so unique. Vintners and brothers Adam and Andrew Mariani harvest varietals such as riesling, sylvaner and St. Laurent, not traditionally found in the pinot-heavy Sonoma region. Kelly, their sister and head chef, manages the food program at the restored hacienda and lets their garden dictate the rotating tasting menu. Even some of the dishware is fired from clay unearthed on the property. Scribe is a true showcase for the beauty of California and the ingenuity of its people.

PICNIC PLATTER

Californians love the start of beach season. The Pacific Coast Highway generally becomes a car park so once you find a spot, it's a hassle to leave. This platter is easy to transport in a cooler for a summer day on the beach.

---

3 different types of cheese: hard, semi-hard, soft (milx of mild, pungent and nutty)

3 different types of charcuterie: whole salamis and sliced options

3 types seasonal fresh fruit: summer stone fruit or melon, autumn persimmons or pomegranates

2 types crackers: oat, crispy

1 rustic bread, sliced or torn

2 types nuts: pistachios, almonds, cashews

1 local honey

serves 8–10   **prep** 5 mins   **cook** none

Key to a great board is to choose different textures and flavours that ultimately will complement each other. For example, a very pungent cheese can be nicely rounded out with a floral peach or honey. A dark yeasty bread stands up to a spicy, richer sliced soppressata. This is more of a guideline to help you pick a varied spread. Mix in some dried fruits as well when peak season fresh fruits aren't as abundant.

MELON & CUCUMBER SALAD

When the weather gets hot, this salad will cool you off. It's apparent when melon has arrived at the farmers' market because most of the chefs in the state will have it on their menu in some form to celebrate the iconic summer flavours.

2 teaspoons sesame seeds

½ teaspoon coriander seeds

½ teaspoon cumin seeds

3 tablespoons smoked almonds

170 g (6 oz) mascarpone, whisked until smooth

½ small honeydew melon, rind and seeds removed, finely sliced

2 lemon cucumbers or other summer variety, finely sliced

2 small kohlrabi, peeled and finely sliced

Sea salt flakes

Extra virgin olive oil, for drizzling

Juice of 1 lime, to taste

10 finger limes, halved and segments scraped (or segmented and chopped lime)

2 handfuls spicy or floral flowering herbs or microgreens

serves 4   **prep** 10 mins   **cook** 5 mins

Toast all the seeds in a small frying pan over medium–low heat for 3–5 minutes until fragrant. Add the almonds and toast for another minute. Remove from the pan and leave to cool. Roughly chop or smash with a mortar and pestle.

Swipe the mascarpone on the bottom of a large platter or around the sides of a large shallow serving bowl. Layer the melon, cucumbers and kohlrabi, then sprinkle the seed mix all over. Season with salt and a drizzle of olive oil. Squeeze a little lime juice to taste. Top with finger limes and flowering herbs.

FORAGING

Foraging for wild plants and herbs in the Golden State's backyard is quite an extraordinary Californian experience. An excursion with Pascal Baudar, a wild food researcher and author, reveals lots of naturally growing edibles, such as lamb's quarters (wild spinach), mustard, currants and sweet white clover to name a few. Pascal mindfully forages in order to maintain balance within the environment, which is the essence of wildcrafting. His appreciation for wild edibles and how they can be prepared with various culinary techniques will leave you excited to get back to the kitchen to make a meal with your foraged bounty.

POTATO SALAD WITH GREENS & SMOKED FISH

With Californians' outdoor lifestyles, it's good to have dishes that travel well. This salad falls into that category as it works slightly warm, room temperature or even cold. The sturdier purslane will hold up. If using watercress, mix in at the last minute for a picnic.

680 g (1½ lb) baby potatoes, halved if large

Sea salt, sea salt flakes and freshly ground black pepper

60 ml (2 fl oz/¼ cup) extra virgin olive oil, plus extra to serve

3 tablespoons wholegrain mustard

3 tablespoons mayonnaise

1 teaspoon celery seeds

150 g (5½ oz) Half Sour Pickles, finely diced, plus 2 tablespoons brine (see page 209)

2 celery stalks, finely chopped

4 large eggs

170 g (6 oz) smoked fish, such as trout, mackerel or sardines, flaked

½ bunch purslane, miners lettuce or watercress, leaves and small sprigs picked

serves 6–8   **prep** 5 mins   **cook** 20 mins

Place the potatoes in a medium saucepan and fill with enough cold water to cover by 5 cm (2 in). Add salt and bring to the boil. Reduce to a gentle simmer and cook for 8–12 minutes until tender when pierced.

Meanwhile, place the olive oil, mustard, mayonnaise, celery seeds, ½ teaspoon salt and ½ teaspoon pepper in a large bowl and whisk to combine. Add the pickles, brine and celery. When the potatoes are ready, remove with a slotted spoon and lay on a clean dish towel to dry slightly. Transfer the potatoes to the bowl while they are still hot and toss to combine. Leave to cool, tossing occasionally to let the flavours fully absorb.

Meanwhile, bring the pan back to the boil. Prepare an ice bath. Lower the eggs into the water and simmer for 8 minutes. Transfer the eggs to the ice bath. Gently crack the eggs all around and leave to cool just enough to handle. Peel and slice the eggs.

Add the smoked fish and purslane to the salad and toss lightly to combine. Top with the eggs, a drizzle of olive oil and season.

SMASHED CUCUMBERS

Refreshing and quick, this dish can be eaten as a side with other dishes or as an afternoon snack.

---

6 short cucumbers (600 g/
1 lb 5 oz), cut crossways into
thirds

1 teaspoon sea salt

3 tablespoons rice vinegar

2 tablespoons neutral oil

2 teaspoons toasted sesame oil

2 teaspoons granulated sugar

2 teaspoons fish sauce

2 Thai chilies, finely sliced

1 garlic clove, grated

Toasted sesame seeds, to serve

Handful of Thai basil, to serve

serves 4   **prep** 5 mins + 30 mins to salt   **cook** none

Gently smash the cucumber segments with a rolling pin or the side of a chef's knife. Break into pieces where the cucumbers split. Place in a colander over a bowl and season with salt. Toss to combine, then set aside to drain for at least 30 minutes.

Add the remaining ingredients to a large bowl and whisk until combined. Add the drained cucumbers to the bowl and toss well. Top with the seeds and torn basil to serve.

SUMMER BEAN SALAD WITH SPINACH

Produce such as heirloom spinach and summer beans from the farmers' markets are so sweet and flavourful already, you don't have to do much. The breadcrumbs and cheese give a savoury balance and crunch.

80 ml (2½ fl oz/⅓ cup) extra virgin olive oil

4 anchovy fillets

40 g (1½ oz/½ cup) fresh breadcrumbs

4 garlic cloves, 2 grated, 2 smashed

Grated zest of 1 lemon

1 teaspoon chilli flakes

340 g (12 oz) mixed summer beans

1 bunch of heirloom spinach

Sea salt flakes and freshly ground black pepper

15 g (½ oz) parmesan cheese, grated

serves 4   **prep** 5 mins   **cook** 15 mins

Place 3 tablespoons of the olive oil and the anchovies in a large frying pan over medium heat and cook for 5 minutes, stirring until the anchovies have melted. Add the breadcrumbs and cook for another 5 minutes, or until the crumbs are golden. Stir in the grated garlic, lemon zest and chilli flakes and cook for another minute. Transfer to a bowl, lightly season with salt and wipe out the pan.

Return the pan to medium–high heat. Add the remaining olive oil and the smashed garlic. Cook the beans and spinach in 2 separate batches, about 2 minutes for the beans and 1 minute for the spinach, or until just bright and crisp tender. Season with salt and pepper.

Transfer the vegetables to a large platter and top with the breadcrumbs and grated cheese.

GRILLED AVOCADO & LOBSTER SALAD

Japanese flavours and ingredients are so subtle and clean, they are well suited for this lobster salad. And since it's California, why not grill an avocado for a hit of smokiness to balance out the sweet lobster?

---

60 g (2½ oz) unsalted butter

1 tablespoon togarashi (Japanese 7-spice)

Handful of shiso sprigs or 6 large leaves, chopped

1 bunch of chives, chopped

Sea salt flakes

2 small whole lobsters, split through the centre, head matter removed (if liked – see note)

2 small avocados, halved and stoned

Grated zest and juice of 1 lemon

1 short cucumber, finely sliced

1 tablespoon toasted sesame seeds

Thin rice cakes or crunchy potato chips to serve

serves 6–8   **prep** 15 mins   **cook** 10 mins

Place the butter, togarashi, half the shiso and half the chives in a small saucepan over low heat to melt. Stir to combine the flavours and season. Remove from the heat.

Preheat the griller (broiler) to high. Lightly brush the cut sides of the lobster with the butter mixture and grill for 3 minutes, cut side down, with the claws positioned in the hotter areas. Flip and brush again with more of the butter. Grill for another 3 minutes, or until the meat is just cooked through. Transfer to a board and cool slightly.

Brush the cut side of the avocados lightly with the butter mixture and season. Grill for 1–2 minutes on each side until charred in spots. Remove from the heat and cool slightly. Mash half the avocado and place in a large bowl. Add the lemon juice, 1 teaspoon salt and stir to combine. Chop the remaining avocado and add to the bowl. Set aside.

Crack the lobster claws when cool enough to handle. Remove the claw and tail meat and chop into bite-sized pieces. Transfer to the bowl with the avocado. Add half the remaining herbs, the lemon zest, cucumber and half the sesame seeds and gently mix to combine. Top with the remaining herbs, seeds and season with salt. Serve with rice cakes or potato chips.

Notes: The tomalley (head matter) is really sweet and creamy when cooked. It may not be for everyone but the rich flavour is worth a try. If using, start the lobster on the grill, cut side up, so that the tomalley cooks. Scoop out before flipping and reserve to stir into the salad.

CRISPY RICE SUSHI

Sushi in California is so common now that regular supermarkets have a dedicated team to make the little boxes for takeaway. This version is a bit more special with the added texture of the crispy rice to contrast the fresh fish.

---

190 g (6½ oz) sushi rice

1 tablespoon rice wine vinegar

1 tablespoon granulated sugar

1½ teaspoons sea salt

280 g (10 oz) skinless sushi-grade fish or 20 pieces uni (sea urchin) or combo

3 tablespoons soy sauce

Wasabi or lemon juice, to taste (optional)

Rapeseed or other neutral oil, for cooking

Fragrant herbs, such as chopped spring (green) onions, shiso, sorrel, spicy or citrusy flowers, to garnish

serves 4   **prep** 20 mins   **cook** 35 mins

Rinse and drain the rice 10 times, or until the water runs clear. Drain well and transfer to a rice cooker or small saucepan and add 240 ml (8 fl oz) water. Cook according to the rice cooker's manual. If using a pan, bring to the boil over medium–high heat, cover, reduce the heat to low and cook for 10 minutes, or until tender and the water is absorbed. Remove from the heat and leave, covered, for 5 minutes. Transfer to a large shallow bowl.

Meanwhile, place the vinegar, sugar and salt in a small saucepan and heat over medium–low heat, stirring for 1–2 minutes until just dissolved. Sprinkle over the rice and fluff with a rice paddle or a wooden spoon. Cool to room temperature.

Slice the fish into 20 pieces, about 7 mm (¼ in) thick and about 4 x 4 cm (1½ x 1½ in) pieces or similar. Chill until ready to assemble. Mix the soy and wasabi or lemon juice to taste. Set aside.

Lightly oil a small piece of plastic wrap. With wet hands, portion the rice into 20 (2 tablespoons/20 g/¾ oz), rewetting hands as needed to prevent sticking. One at a time, wrap the rice in plastic, form in a tight ball and press down lightly to form a 1 cm (½ in) thick disc, about 5 cm (2 in) wide.

Heat a large cast-iron frying pan over medium–high heat. Add 3 tablespoons of oil. Place half the rice discs in the pan and cook for 4–5 minutes on each side until golden and just crispy, adding more oil and adjusting the heat for the second side as necessary. Transfer to a plate lined with kitchen paper and repeat.

Place the fish on top of the rice and brush with the soy mixture or serve on the side. Top with herbs.

DINNER

Strolling through local grocers in California offers a glimpse into the variety of the state's culinary lifestyles. Whether a carnivore or pescatarian, vegan or gluten free, there's something for everyone – seasonal spot prawns from Santa Barbara, wild harvested seaweed from the Sonoma coast, happily raised and well-fed pigs from Valley Center or heirloom grains from Los Osos. Paired with the local rainbow of seasonal produce, dinners in California are deliciously well rounded, and these recipes – pizza topped with ricotta and summer squash, Korean-style BBQ short ribs and leaf-wrapped grilled fish – offer a taste of that.

SALMON BURGER

Local wild salmon has pristine flavour and colour. The richness of the fish pairs well with the punchy herbs and pickles.

Grated zest and juice of
1 lemon

1 small shallot, diced small

2 celery stalks, diced small,
plus inner celery leaves

1 large egg, lightly beaten

2 tablespoons wholegrain
mustard

110 g (4 oz) mayonnaise

10 g (¼ oz) fresh breadcrumbs

680 g (1½ lb) skinless salmon,
cut into bite-sized pieces

3 tablespoons extra virgin
olive oil

50 g (1¾ oz) soft herbs, such as
parsley, chervil, chives, wood
or regular sorrel

150 g (5½ oz) Half Sour Pickles,
sliced, plus extra to serve (see
page 209)

4 soft buns, toasted

Sea salt flakes and freshly
ground black pepper

serves 4   **prep** 15 mins   **cook** 10 min

Place the lemon zest, shallot, diced celery, egg, mustard, 1 tablespoon of the mayonnaise and the breadcrumbs in a food processor and pulse to combine. Add the salmon, 2 teaspoons salt and 1 teaspoon pepper and pulse a few times just until everything is lightly mixed. Do not over-process. There should still be some larger pieces of salmon. Form the mixture into 4 patties.

Heat a large cast-iron frying pan over medium–high heat. Add 2 tablespoons of the olive oil and cook the patties for 3–4 minutes on each side until deep golden and just cooked through.

Place the celery leaves and herbs in a medium bowl and lightly dress with 1 tablespoon of lemon juice and the remaining olive oil. Season. Spread the remaining mayonnaise on the bottom bun, top with the salmon patty, herb salad, pickles and the other half of the bun. Serve with more pickles, if liked.

GREEN POZOLE

This comforting stew develops even more flavour as it sits. It can be made a day ahead and reheated. The variety of accompaniments finishes off this dish with bright notes and good texture.

900 g (2 lb) pork shoulder, cut into 5 cm (2 in) pieces

Sea salt flakes and freshly ground black pepper

900 g (2 lb) tomatillos, husked

1 poblano chilli pepper

1 white onion, quartered, 1 quarter finely diced to serve

1 tablespoon extra virgin olive oil

2 garlic cloves, smashed

2 fresh bay leaves

350 ml (12 fl oz) Mexican-style beer

950 ml (32 fl oz) chicken stock

2 teaspoons dried oregano, plus extra to serve

2 x 400 g (14 oz) tins hominy, drained (found in speciality stores)

Accompaniments:

Shredded cabbage, sliced radish, diced onion, chopped avocado, toasted pumpkin seeds, sliced jalapeños, tortilla chips, oregano

serves 4   **prep** 15 mins
cook 30 mins + 2 plus hours to braise

Heat the griller (broiler) to high.

Season the pork all over with salt and pepper and set aside.

Place the tomatillos, poblano and 3 onion quarters on a baking sheet on the top rack and grill (broil) for 8–10 minutes, rotating a few times, until charred in spots. Transfer to a board. When cool enough to handle, discard the stem and seeds of the poblano, then chop the poblano, tomatillos and onions and set aside.

Preheat the oven to 150°C (300°F).

Heat the olive oil in a large casserole dish over medium–high heat. Add the pork in a single layer and cook for 3–5 minutes on each side until browned. Add the garlic, bay leaves and beer, scraping up the brown bits on the bottom of the dish. Add the reserved roasted vegetables, the stock, oregano, 1 tablespoon salt and 1 teaspoon pepper. Bring to a gentle simmer, cover with lid and transfer to the oven. Braise for at least 2 hours, or until the pork is fork tender. Skim off excess fat. Stir in the hominy and return to the oven for 30 minutes, or until the hominy is heated through.

Serve hot with accompaniments of choice.

BITTER GREENS SALAD

Winter bitter greens need complementary flavours such as earthy beets, sweet squid, floral meyer lemons, salty olives and fresh herbs. The colours of this salad are as stunning as the taste.

8 small beets

125 ml (4 fl oz/½ cup) extra virgin olive oil

450 g (1 lb) squid (mixed bodies and tentacles)

40 g (1½ oz/½ cup) fresh breadcrumbs

Grated zest and juice of 1 meyer lemon

2 small heads bitter greens, such as Treviso, radicchio and/or endive

30 g (1 oz) bottarga, grated

½ small red onion, very finely sliced

75 g (2¾ oz) green olives, pitted

25 g (1 oz) mixed soft herbs such as parsley, chervil, tarragon and chives

Sea salt flakes and freshly ground black pepper

serves 4   **prep** 10 mins   **cook** 55 mins

Preheat the oven to 220°C (425°F). Wrap the beets in foil and roast on the middle rack of the oven for 45 minutes, or until tender when pierced with a knife. Unwrap and cool, then peel the skins and tops off, slice finely and set aside.

Heat 2 tablespoons of the olive oil in a cast-iron frying pan over medium–high heat. Season the squid and sear for 2 minutes on each side for the bodies and 1 minute on each side for the tentacles. Press down on the squid with a spatula for even contact and browning. Transfer to a plate.

Wipe out the pan and return to medium heat. Add 2 tablespoons of the olive oil and stir in the breadcrumbs until lightly coated. Cook, stirring frequently, for 5 minutes, or until golden brown. Set aside.

Place the lemon zest, juice, the remaining olive oil, ½ teaspoon salt and ½ teaspoon pepper in a bowl and whisk to combine.

Divide the greens, beets and squid among 4 plates. Drizzle with the dressing. Garnish with the breadcrumbs, bottarga, red onion, olives and herbs. Season lightly.

CRISPY CHICKEN WITH BEANS

In the summertime, try this dish with fresh shelling beans. Fresh beans have the perfect bite, do not require soaking and will cook much quicker than their dried cousins.

---

4 whole chicken legs

Sea salt flakes and freshly ground black pepper

2 fresh bay leaves

1 small onion, halved

3 garlic cloves, 1 unpeeled, 2 finely sliced

225 g (8 oz) dried butter beans, soaked overnight and drained

5 whole black peppercorns

80 ml (2½ fl oz/⅓ cup) extra virgin olive oil

2 celery stalks, plus inner leaves, stalks finely chopped

10 g (¼ oz) parsley leaves

1 preserved lemon, rinsed, rind finely chopped (see page 217)

serves 4   **prep** 5 mins + 8 hours/overnight for soaking beans   **cook** 50 mins

Preheat the oven to 200°C (400°F). Season the chicken legs all over with salt and pepper and set aside.

Toast the bay leaves, onion and unpeeled garlic in a casserole dish over medium–high heat for 4–5 minutes until charred in spots. Add the beans, peppercorns, 2 teaspoons salt and enough water to cover the beans by 5 cm (2 in). Bring to a gentle simmer and cook for 30 minutes, or until just tender, checking halfway through that there is enough water to cover the beans.

Meanwhile, heat a large cast-iron frying pan over medium–high heat. Add 2 tablespoons of the olive oil, then place the chicken, skin side down, pressing down to ensure even contact. Cook for 8–10 minutes until the skin is golden brown and starting to get crispy. Flip the chicken and place the pan in the oven for another 11–13 minutes until the chicken is almost cooked through. Turn on the oven griller (broiler) and grill (broil) the chicken for 2 minutes, or until the skin is crisp. Leave to rest on a plate.

Return the pan with 1 tablespoon of the olive oil to medium heat. Add the sliced garlic and cook for 1–2 minutes, stirring a few times until just golden and crisp. Transfer to a bowl and set aside. Reduce the heat to low. Use a slotted spoon to transfer the beans to the pan and toss.

Add the chopped celery, celery and parsley leaves, preserved lemon and the remaining olive oil to the garlic chips and season lightly. Toss gently.

Divide the beans among 4 shallow bowls and spoon the lemon herb mixture on top. Serve with 1 chicken leg each.

PIZZA

The key to a great pizza is a light touch with the dough and a very hot oven. The simple base allows for the sweetness of the vegetables and aromatics to come through. If liked, substitute squash for other finely sliced vegetables, such as mushrooms.

450 g (1 lb) fresh pizza dough

flour, for dusting

340 g (12 oz) mixed summer squash

½ small red onion, finely sliced

Grated zest and juice of 1 lemon

2 tablespoons extra virgin olive oil, plus extra for drizzling

170 g (6 oz) ricotta

170 g (6 oz) mascarpone

40 g (1½ oz) parmesan cheese, grated, plus extra to serve (optional)

2 garlic cloves, grated

Medium polenta, for dusting

25 g (1 oz) mixed soft herbs, such as nasturtium leaves and flowers, marjoram, chives and parsley

Sea salt flakes and freshly ground black pepper

serves 4 **prep** 10 mins + 30 mins resting **cook** 20 mins

Divide the dough in half and gently form into 2 balls. Dust lightly with flour, cover with a clean dish towel and rest for 30 minutes.

Preheat the oven to the highest setting and place a pizza stone or upside down baking sheet on the bottom shelf to heat.

Finely slice the squash about 3 mm (⅛ in) thick, then transfer to a colander and toss with ½ teaspoon salt. Leave to drain for 10 minutes, then pat dry with a clean dish towel and transfer to a bowl. Add the onion, lemon zest, 1 tablespoon of lemon juice, the olive oil, 1 teaspoon salt and ½ teaspoon pepper and toss to combine.

Place the ricotta, mascarpone, parmesan, garlic, ½ teaspoon salt, and ½ teaspoon pepper in another bowl and whisk to combine.

Generously dust an upside-down baking sheet with polenta. Stretch the first piece of dough on a lightly floured work surface to an oval, about 33 x 23 cm (13 x 9 in), leaving the borders slightly thicker. If the dough is offering resistance, leave to rest for 10 minutes longer. Lay the base on the baking sheet, shaking once or twice to make sure it moves freely. Dot and spread half the cheese mixture over the dough. Lift half the vegetables out and place on the cheese. Transfer the pizza to the hot pizza stone and cook for 8–10 minutes until the crust is deeply golden and puffed. Transfer to a wire rack and repeat with the second piece of dough letting the oven and baking sheet come back up to temperature before cooking. Serve with the herbs, a drizzle of olive oil and extra parmesan, if liked.

GRILLED STEAK WITH TOMATO SALAD

Californians are fond of their summer tomatoes and savour every minute of the seasonal fruit. The juices and seeds are such a flavourful part of this dish, so don't discard them.

680 g (1½ lb) hangar or onglet steak

Sea salt flakes and freshly ground black pepper

1 bunch of tarragon, leaves picked

60 g (2½ oz) unsalted butter, softened

5 cm (2 in) piece of fresh horseradish, peeled and grated

450 g (1 lb) mixed colour and size heirloom tomatoes

3 thick slices country loaf

1 tablespoon extra virgin olive oil, plus extra for brushing

½ small red onion, very finely sliced

8 small radishes, very finely sliced

serves 4 **prep** 10 mins **cook** 15 mins

Season the steak all over with salt and pepper and set aside.

Preheat the barbecue grill to high. Alternatively, use a stovetop chargrill pan and heat over medium–high heat.

Finely chop half the tarragon, place in a bowl, add the butter and 3 tablespoons horseradish and mash with a fork to combine. Set aside.

Slice the larger tomatoes into wedges and halve or quarter smaller tomatoes. Cherry tomatoes can stay whole, if liked. Reserve the juices and tomatoes in a large bowl.

Lightly brush the bread with olive oil, then grill for 2–3 minutes on each side until charred in spots. Transfer to a wire rack and top with a light sprinkle of salt.

Lightly brush the meat with oil and grill for 3–4 minutes until deeply browned. Flip and repeat. Transfer to the wire rack, top with the herbed butter and leave to rest.

Cut or tear the bread slices into bite-sized pieces and place in the bowl with the tomatoes. Add half the onion, the olive oil, 1 teaspoon salt and ½ teaspoon pepper and toss to combine. Transfer to a platter.

Finely slice the steak and place on top of the tomato salad. Top with the radishes, remaining onion and tarragon. Finish with a light sprinkling of grated horseradish and season.

CRAB FRIED RICE

Using the stems of Asian greens is a great way to add crunch and freshness to the rice. Try it with any market greens with the same structure.

8 large egg whites

75 ml (2½ fl oz) rapeseed or other neutral oil

1 bunch of Chinese greens (gai lan, choy sum or bok choy) leaves separated, stems sliced 5 mm (2 in) thick

2 garlic cloves, grated

5 cm (2 in) piece of fresh ginger, peeled and grated

½ bunch of spring (green) onions, sliced, whites and greens separated

390 g (14 oz) cooked long-grain white rice, cold (see note)

225 g (8 oz) cooked crabmeat

Sea salt flakes and ground white pepper

serves 4 **prep** 15 mins + 30 mins if need to prepare rice **cook** 10 mins

Whisk the egg whites in a bowl, then season with 1 teaspoon salt and ½ teaspoon white pepper. Set aside.

Heat a large cast-iron or non-stick frying pan over medium heat. Add 1 tablespoon of the oil and swirl to coat. Add the leaves of the greens, half the garlic and season. Sauté for 2–3 minutes until the greens are bright and just wilted. Transfer to a plate and set aside.

Return the pan to medium heat. Add 3 tablespoons of the oil, the remaining garlic, ginger, spring onion whites and the stems of the greens. Season with 1½ teaspoons salt and cook for 1 minute until fragrant. Add the cold rice and stir to break up any clumps and coat the grains. Cook for 5 minutes, or until the rice is heated through. Stir in the crab meat and cook for 2 minutes, or until warmed. Make a very large well and add the remaining oil. Add the reserved egg whites and cook for 1–2 minutes until just set, gently folding so the raw egg touches the bottom of the pan. Lightly break apart and combine with the rice. Serve, topped with the reserved greens and spring onion.

Note: This recipe is a great use of leftover rice. If you don't have leftover rice, cook 190 g (6½ oz) dry. Rinse and drain the rice 10 times, or until the water is mainly clear. Drain well and transfer to a rice cooker or small saucepan and add 240 ml (8 fl oz) water. Cook according to rice cooker's manual. If using a saucepan, bring to the boil over medium–high heat. Cover and reduce the heat to medium–low and simmer for 10–12 minutes until tender and the water is absorbed. Remove from the heat, cover and leave for 5 minutes. Transfer to a small metal baking sheet or baking dish and cool in the freezer for 20 minutes before using.

THE GOLDEN STATE

Though the nickname was coined after the discovery of gold in 1848, it is also a testament to the golden majesty that radiates across California. From the fields of wild poppies blossoming after spring rain to the glowing Pacific coast sunsets to the iconic colour of the Golden Gate Bridge, the magical hue washes over California and dazzles the senses.

SPRING CARBONARA

Santa Barbara *uni* can be perfectly sweet and briny at the same time. Taking advantage of its tender texture, it's made into sauces for pasta the way carbonara is. The earthy green from the nettles turns this dish into a surf and turf of sorts.

---

1 large bunch nettles (about 280 g/10 oz)

3 tablespoons extra virgin olive oil

70 g (2½ oz) spring green garlic, finely chopped

185 g (6½ oz) uni (sea urchin)

140 g (5 oz) shelled fresh garden peas

450 g (1 lb) long pasta, such as tagliatelle or pappardelle

60 g (2 oz) cured salmon roe

Grated zest of 1 meyer lemon

Flowering herbs, such as borage, onion flower or spring (green) onion, to garnish

Sea salt flakes and freshly ground black pepper

serves 4 **prep** 10 mins **cook** 10 mins

Wear thick gloves to work with nettles. Pick or snip the leaves and discard the stems. You should have 90 g (3 oz) leaves.

Heat a large frying pan over medium heat. Add the olive oil, the garlic, ½ teaspoon salt and ½ teaspoon pepper and cook for 1 minute, or until starting to soften. Stir in the nettles and season lightly. Cook for another 1–2 minutes until fully wilted. Transfer the mixture to a food processor, add all but 8 pieces of uni and process until the uni is smooth and the greens are chopped. Scrape into a large bowl.

Bring a large pan of salted water to the boil. Place the peas in a sieve and lower into the water for 30 seconds to quickly blanch. Set aside. Add the pasta and cook according to the pack instructions, or until just al dente.

When the pasta is ready, use tongs to immediately transfer it into the uni mixture. Toss thoroughly with another splash of pasta water, then divide among 4 shallow bowls. Top with the reserved peas, remaining uni, salmon roe, lemon zest and herbs. Season lightly.

Note: If nettles are unavailable, substitute 90 g (3 oz) of any soft herb, such as parsley, chives, nasturtiums and chervil.

KIMCHI SEAFOOD STEW

This stew is a lighter version of what you would order in one of the numerous Korean restaurants in Los Angeles. It comes together quickly for an easy dinner.

450 g (1 lb) skinless ocean white fish or snapper fillets, cut into 5 cm (2 in) pieces

Sea salt flakes and freshly ground black pepper

950 ml (32 fl oz) vegetable stock (see page 197)

225 g (8 oz) kimchi, chopped

16 baby turnips, greens reserved (170 g/6 oz)

75 g (2¾ oz) beech mushrooms, trimmed

35 g (1¼ oz) enoki mushrooms, trimmed

350 g (12½ oz) silken extra-firm tofu, cut into 4 pieces

20 small clams, scrubbed

4 spring (green) onions, cut into 5 cm (2 in) pieces

Cooked jasmine rice, to serve

serves 4 **prep** 10 mins **cook** 20 mins

Season the fish and set aside.

Combine the stock and kimchi in a large saucepan and bring to the boil. Reduce the heat and simmer for 10 minutes. Add the turnips, mushrooms and tofu and cook for 5 minutes. Nestle the fish into the stock and gently layer the clams on top in a single layer. Cover and simmer gently for 3 minutes. Add the turnip greens and spring onions for the last 1–2 minutes of cooking just to wilt. Serve with jasmine rice.

ROASTED WINTER SQUASH BOWL

Some Californians enjoy the change of the seasons to the cooler climates. They pull on their sweaters, head to the market and dig in to the earthy and nutty flavours of autumn squash and mushrooms.

---

130 g (4½ oz) hazelnuts

900 g (2 lb) pumpkin (winter squash), seeded and cut into thick wedges

450 g (1 lb) mixed mushrooms, ends trimmed, left in large clusters or whole

1 small red onion, cut into 8 wedges

10 thyme sprigs

2 lemons, 1 finely sliced, zest and juice of other

185 ml (6 fl oz/¾ cup) extra virgin olive oil, plus extra for drizzling

1 bulb garlic, halved crossways

185 g (6½ oz) wheat berries, rinsed

1 small bunch of rocket (arugula)

Sea salt flakes and freshly ground black pepper

serves 4   **prep** 10 mins   **cook** 1 hour 5 mins

Preheat the oven to 180°C (350°F). Toast the hazelnuts on a baking sheet for 10–15 minutes until deep golden and the skins are starting to split. Leave to cool slightly, then use a dish towel to rub as much of the skins off as possible. Roughly chop. Wipe off the baking sheet and return to the oven on the bottom rack. Increase the heat to 220°C (425°F).

Add the squash, mushrooms, onion, 5 thyme sprigs and the lemon slices to a large bowl and toss with 60 ml (2 fl oz/¼ cup) of the olive oil. Season with 2 teaspoons salt and 1 teaspoon pepper. Transfer to the preheated baking sheet. Place the garlic halves on a small piece of foil and drizzle with olive oil. Join the halves back together and wrap tightly. Place in the corner of the baking sheet. Roast the vegetables on the bottom rack for 45–50 minutes until the squash is tender and the vegetables are caramelised in spots, tossing every 15 minutes.

Meanwhile, bring a small saucepan of salted water to the boil. Add the wheat berries and simmer for 40 minutes, or until tender yet still retain some bite. Drain.

Carefully remove the garlic halves. Squeeze out the roasted cloves into a large bowl, mash and discard the skins. Add the lemon zest and juice, the leaves from the remaining thyme sprigs, the remaining olive oil, ½ teaspoon salt and ¼ teaspoon pepper and whisk to combine. Add the wheat berries and toss well.

Serve the vegetables with the dressed wheat berries, rocket and hazelnuts. Season lightly.

GRILLED PRAWNS & CREAMED CORN

This dish is a Californian play on prawn and grits. Local Santa Barbara spot prawns are ideal in sweetness to marry with the summer corn.

6 mint sprigs, leaves torn

6 marjoram sprigs, leaves torn

1 jalapeño chilli, finely sliced

1 garlic clove, grated

60 ml (2 fl oz/¼ cup) white wine

75 ml (2½ fl oz) extra virgin olive oil

16 whole spot prawns (shrimp) or tiger prawns (about 1.2 kg/ 2 lb 10 oz), deveined through the shell

4 corn-on-the-cobs (about 900 g/2 lb), husked

60 g (2½ oz) unsalted butter

2 clusters (300 g/10½ oz) beech mushrooms, ends trimmed and broken into smaller pieces

2 small leeks, white and light green parts chopped

Sea salt flakes and freshly ground black pepper

Lime wedges, to serve

serves 4 **prep** 15 mins **cook** 20 mins

In a shallow bowl or baking dish, combine half the mint and half the marjoram, the jalapeño, garlic, wine, 60 ml (2 fl oz/¼ cup) of the olive oil, 1 teaspoon salt and ½ teaspoon pepper. Toss the prawns in the marinade and then set aside.

One at a time, lay the corn flat and carefully cut off one side of the kernels. Rotate and repeat on the remaining 3 sides. Transfer the kernels to a bowl. Stand the cobs upright in the bowl and use a spoon to scrape any remaining juice into the bowl. Repeat with the remaining cobs. Transfer half the corn mixture to a food processor and blitz for 30 seconds, or until it is slightly creamy but not fully smooth. Set aside. reserve the whole corn.

Heat a large cast-iron frying pan over medium–high heat. Add the remaining 1 tablespoon of the olive oil, 2 tablespoons of the butter, the mushrooms, ½ teaspoon salt and ½ teaspoon pepper and cook for 5–8 minutes until the mushrooms are golden. Reduce the heat to medium, add the remaining butter and leeks and cook for 3–5 minutes until the leeks have just softened. Stir in the puréed corn and 60 ml (2 fl oz/¼ cup) water and reduce to a gentle simmer for 2 minutes. Stir in the reserved whole kernels and juices and season. Cook for 1 minute longer. Turn off the heat and cover to keep warm.

Heat the barbecue grill or a stovetop chargrill pan to medium–high. Remove the prawns from the marinade and grill for 3–4 minutes until charred in spots and just cooked through, turning once.

Spoon the creamed corn into 4 bowls. Top with the grilled prawns. Tear the remaining herbs and sprinkle over. Serve with lime wedges.

CALIFORNIA SMASHED BURGERS

A popular concept in California is to be able to order a burrito, sandwich or burger without the outer carb layer. If you are able to find a crisp variety of lettuce at your local farmers' market, the crunch is so satisfying that you might not miss the bun.

---

675 g (1½ lb) minced (ground) beef (80:20 meat to fat ratio)

2 tablespoons yellow American mustard

50 g (1¾ oz) Half Sour Pickles, chopped (see page 209)

55 g (2 oz) mayonnaise

65 g (2¼ oz) ketchup

4 teaspoons rapeseed or other neutral oil

100 g (3½ oz) cheddar cheese, finely sliced

1 head crisp green lettuce, such as iceberg, leaves separated

1 large tomato ketchup, finely sliced

Sea salt flakes and freshly ground black pepper

½ small red onion, very finely sliced

serves 4 **prep** 5 mins **cook** 35 mins

Divide the beef into 8 portions and gently form into eight 10 cm (4 in) diameter patties. Season the patties, then lightly brush each side with the mustard.

To make the sauce, combine the pickles, mayonnaise and ketchup in a small bowl and stir well.

Heat a large cast-iron frying pan over medium–high heat until very hot. Add 1 teaspoon of the oil and swirl to coat. Add 2 patties and immediately place a slightly smaller heavy pan in the pan to weigh down the patties. Cook for 2 minutes, then remove the weight and flip the patties, immediately returning the weight, and cook for another 1 minute. Remove the weight, top each patty with 15 g (½ oz) cheddar and flip the top pan over so it forms a domed lid. Cook for 1 minute, or until the burgers are cooked to the desired doneness and the cheese is melted. Repeat with the remaining burger patties and cheese.

To assemble the burgers, stack 2 burger patties onto a couple of lettuce leaves. Top with tomatoes, salt and pepper, onion and a dollop of the sauce. Finish with 2 more lettuce leaves.

BBQ SHORT RIBS

Korean-style short ribs cook quickly on the barbecue grill with the slight char adding a good depth of flavour. The lightly dressed salad cleanses the palate nicely.

1 bunch of spring (green) onions, half roughly chopped, half finely sliced

1 small Asian pear, peeled, cored and roughly chopped

3 garlic cloves

1 tablespoon grated ginger

125 ml (4½ fl oz/½ cup) soy sauce

60 ml (2 fl oz/¼ cup) rice vinegar

40 g (1½ oz) light brown sugar

3 tablespoons toasted sesame oil

150 g (5½ oz) kimchi radish, finely sliced plus 3 tablespoons liquid

1.4 kg (3 lb 1 oz) Korean-style short ribs (5–10mm/¼–½ in thick)

Sea salt flakes and freshly ground black pepper

2 tablespoons rapeseed or other neutral oil, plus extra for brushing

2 heads small gem lettuce, cut crossways into strips

1 tablespoon toasted sesame seeds

serves 4 **prep** 15 mins + 4 hours/overnight for marinating **cook** 5 mins

Place the chopped spring onions, pear, garlic, ginger, soy sauce, vinegar, sugar, 2 tablespoons of the sesame oil and 2 tablespoons of the kimchi liquid in a food processor or blender and purée until smooth.

Lightly rub the short ribs all over with salt and pepper. Place in a large baking dish or sealable plastic bag. Pour the marinade over and chill for at least 4 hours, or overnight.

Remove the ribs from the marinade at least 30 minutes before cooking. Heat the barbecue grill to high.

Lightly brush the meat with oil and grill for about 2 minutes on each side until lightly charred and cooked to medium rare, or your desired doneness. Remove to a rack to rest while you prepare the salad.

Combine the remaining sesame oil, the rapeseed oil and the remaining kimchi liquid in a large bowl. Whisk to combine and season. Add the lettuce, radish and half the spring onions and toss lightly to combine.

Serve the ribs with the salad and topped with the remaining sliced spring onions and sesame seeds.

LEAF-WRAPPED GRILLED FISH

Barbecuing outdoors is the highlight of long summer Californian nights. Using leaves from fruit trees is a great way to impart flavour into grilled foods.

4 large fig or grape leaves

3 tablespoons extra virgin olive oil, plus extra for oiling

2 whole branzino, red snapper or sea bream, about 675–900 g (1½–2 lb) each, cleaned

1 preserved lemon (or other citrus), rinsed, rind sliced into strips, 1 tablespoon liquid (see page 217)

1 small red onion, finely sliced

1 bunch of mixed herbs, such as dill, parsley and chives

Sea salt flakes and freshly ground black pepper

1 bunch of purslane, small sprigs picked, tough stems discarded

serves 4   **prep** 10 mins + 20 mins to soak
cook 16 mins

Soak 6 pieces of kitchen twine, about 36 cm (14 in) long in a bowl of water for at least 20 minutes.

Lay 3 pieces of the twine on a work surface, spaced shorter than the length of the fish. Place 2 leaves side by side with overlap on top of the twine. Lightly oil both sides of the fish and place on the bottom halves of the leaves. Season the fish inside and out with salt and pepper. Place half the preserved lemon, onion and mixed herbs inside the fish, then fold the top halves of the leaves over the fish and use the twine to secure. Repeat with the remaining fish.

Heat a barbecue grill to medium–high and grill for 12–16 minutes, depending on size, flipping once halfway through until charred in spots on the outside and just firm to the touch. Remove to a platter, season lightly and leave to rest.

Whisk the preserved lemon liquid, the olive oil and ½ teaspoon pepper in a large bowl. Add the purslane and toss. Serve alongside the fish.

BAKED SWEET POTATOES

A few sweet potato varieties will turn up in the market during the autumn. If given the opportunity, try the Japanese sweet potatoes with this recipe. If not, the regular orange jewel or garnet variety pairs nicely as well.

4 medium sweet potatoes (about 225 g/8 oz each), halved lengthways

4 tablespoons extra virgin olive oil

170 g (6 oz) natural yoghurt

1 jalapeño chilli, chopped

2 tablespoons chopped dill

Juice of 1 lime

225 g (8 oz) spicy Italian sausage, casings removed

1 small red onion, finely sliced

1 small bunch of kale (about 200 g/7 oz), tough stems removed, leaves finely sliced

Sea salt flakes and freshly ground black pepper

15 g (½ oz) rice cakes, crumbled

serves 4   **prep** 5 mins   **cook** 50 mins

Preheat the oven to 220°C (425°F). Place a baking sheet on the bottom rack.

Rub the potato halves with 2 tablespoons of the olive oil to coat, then place, cut side down, on the hot baking sheet and return to the bottom rack. Bake for 35 minutes, or until tender when pierced with a knife, rotating once halfway through.

Meanwhile, add the yoghurt, jalapeño, dill and 1 tablespoon lime juice to a small bowl. Season and mix to combine. Chill until ready to use.

Heat a large frying pan over medium–high heat. Add another tablespoon of the olive oil and the sausage and cook for 6–8 minutes, breaking up the sausage with a wooden spoon and stirring occasionally, until the meat is browned. Transfer to a bowl and set aside. Add the remaining tablespoon of oil and the onion and cook for 5 minutes, or until lightly golden. Add the kale, season lightly and cook for 2–3 minutes until just wilted. Transfer to the bowl with the meat and toss to combine.

Divide the sausage and kale mixture among the potatoes. Serve with the yoghurt sauce and rice cake crumbles.

PORK TENDERLOIN WITH APRICOTS & GREENS

The floral quality to apricots lends a brightness to this hearty dinner salad. Choose the ripest fruit for the marinade and use firm but ripe to slice. For a variation, try with sweet/tart plums, peaches or nectarines.

680 g (1½ lb) pork tenderloin

Sea salt flakes and freshly ground black pepper

5 apricots, 1 chopped, 4 sliced

3 tablespoons wholegrain mustard

2 tablespoons thyme leaves

2 garlic cloves, grated

90 ml (3 fl oz) extra virgin olive oil

1 small red onion, cut into 8 wedges

2 tablespoons champagne vinegar

225 g (8 oz) mixed greens

serves 4   **prep** 30 mins + 30 mins to 8 hours marinating   **cook** 20 mins + 10 mins rest

Preheat the oven to 220°C (425°F).

Season the pork and set in a shallow baking dish or zip-lock bag. Combine the chopped apricots, 2 tablespoons of the mustard, the thyme, garlic and 2 tablespoons of the olive oil. Marinate for at least 30 minutes at room temperature. If marinating for longer than 30 minutes (up to overnight), chill in the fridge, then remove 30 minutes before cooking.

Heat a large cast-iron frying pan over medium–high heat. Remove the pork from the marinade and pat dry, then season lightly. Add another 2 tablespoons of the olive oil to the pan and sear the pork for 10 minutes, rotating to brown on all sides. Add the onions, tossing once or twice before transferring to the oven to roast for 8–10 minutes for medium rare or until your desired doneness. Remove the pork and onions to a board to rest for 10 minutes before slicing.

Meanwhile, whisk the remaining mustard, the vinegar and the remaining olive oil in a small bowl. Set aside.

Place the mixed greens in a large bowl. Season and add the sliced apricots and roasted red onion. Drizzle half the dressing on top and toss lightly to dress. Slice the pork and divide among 4 plates. Top with the salad and extra dressing, if liked.

DESSERTS

When ingredients are local, fresh and seasonal, dessert can
be as simple as a bowl of perfectly ripe summer cherries. Even
when you want something a little more indulgent, California's
fruits offer a range of flavours – from the explosive tartness of
passionfruit to the nuanced sweetness of a variety of stone
fruits – that raise the profile of classic desserts, such as popsicles,
donuts and skillet cake.

COCONUT POPSICLES

Hot California summer nights need something refreshing to finish off the day. Creamy, sweet, tart and floral, these pops will do the trick.

---

makes 10   **prep** 5 mins + 4½ hours to freeze   **cook** none

PALM SPRINGS DATE POPS

400 ml (13½ fl oz) tinned unsweetened coconut milk

200 g (7 oz) Medjool dates, pitted

50 g (1¾ oz) coconut flakes

2 tablespoons honey

½ teaspoon ground cardamom

Pinch of sea salt flakes

Place all the ingredients in a food processor or blender and purée until smooth. Transfer to popsicle moulds and freeze for 30 minutes before placing in sticks. Return to the freezer to fully set for about 4 hours before unmoulding.

CITRUS CREAMSICLE POPS

400 ml (13½ fl oz) tinned unsweetened coconut milk

125 ml (4 fl oz/½ cup) condensed milk

300 ml (10 fl oz) mixed citrus juice

2 tablespoons mixed citrus zest

Place all the ingredients in a food processor or blender and purée until smooth. Transfer to popsicle moulds and freeze for 30 minutes before placing in sticks. Return to the freezer to fully set for about 4 hours before unmoulding.

STRAWBERRY & VANILLA POPS

170 g (6 oz) strawberries, sliced

55 g (2 oz/¼ cup) granulated sugar

1 vanilla bean, split lengthways and seeds scraped out or 1 teaspoon vanilla bean paste

400 ml (13½ fl oz) tinned sweetened coconut milk

225 g (8 oz) natural yoghurt

Toss the strawberries, sugar and vanilla together in a bowl. Leave for 20 minutes.

Add the milk and yoghurt to a large measuring cup and whisk to combine. Purée the strawberries in a food processor or blender until smooth. Divide among popsicle moulds. Top with the yoghurt mix and swirl. Freeze for 30 minutes before placing in sticks. Return to the freezer for 4 hours until fully set before unmoulding.

DONUTS WITH PASSIONFRUIT CURD

Resembling little fried delicate pillows, these raspberry sugar-coated parcels are tasty even before filling. The addition of creamy curd makes them just that much more special, contrasting the fluffy dough and sugary tart exterior.

240 ml (8 fl oz) milk

440 g (15½ oz) plain (all-purpose) flour, plus extra for dusting

110 g (4 oz/½ cup) granulated sugar

2 teaspoons instant dried yeast

1 teaspoon sea salt

80 g (3 oz) unsalted butter, melted

1 vanilla bean, split lengthways and seeds scraped out

2 large eggs, at room temperature

Rapeseed or other neutral oil for oiling and frying

8 g (¼ oz) freeze-dried raspberries, ground to a powder, to finish

225 g (8 oz) Passionfruit Curd (see page 205)

makes 30   **prep** 30 mins + 2 hours proving
cook 30 mins

Place the milk in a small saucepan and heat over medium–low heat for 4–5 minutes until warm (body temperature). Whisk the flour, 55 g (2 oz/¼ cup) sugar, the yeast and salt in a bowl of a stand mixer to combine. Place the bowl on the stand mixer fitted with a dough hook attachment. With the machine on low, add the milk, butter and vanilla seeds. Add the eggs, one at a time, and mix for 1–2 minutes until combined. Increase the speed to medium and mix for 3 minutes, or until the dough is shiny and wraps around the dough hook.

Transfer the dough to a lightly oiled bowl. Cover loosely with lightly oiled plastic wrap and leave to rise for about 1 hour, or until doubled in size.

Meanwhile, lightly flour a baking sheet and set aside.

Punch down the dough and turn out onto a lightly floured surface. Roll or pat out to 1.5 cm (½ in) thick and punch out rounds using a 5 cm (2 in) cutter. Form the scraps of dough into a ball and leave, covered loosely with plastic wrap for 10 minutes, before rolling and punching out the remaining donuts. Transfer to the prepared sheet leaving 2.5 cm (1 in) space between each. Leave for 30–45 minutes until almost doubled in size.

Heat 7.5 cm (3 in) oil in a large heavy saucepan to 190°C (375°F). Fry the dough in batches, about 1½–2 minutes until golden, turning once. Use a slotted spoon to lift out the donuts and drain on kitchen paper. Repeat. Adjust the heat as necessary to maintain the temperature.

Mix the remaining sugar and the raspberry powder together. While still warm, roll each donut in the sugar mixture until coated. Place the curd in a pastry bag fitted with a 3 mm (⅛ in) tip and squeeze 1–2 teaspoons of the curd into each donut. Serve immediately.

CAMPFIRE COOKIES

Over half the state of California is covered by forests but there are other terrain options for camping such as beach and desert. Overnight in a tent would not be complete without a campfire to keep warm. This cookie is a play on the classic American s'mores.

140 g (5 oz) stoneground wholemeal (whole-wheat) flour

65 g (2¼ oz) plain (all-purpose) flour

1 teaspoon baking powder

½ teaspoon baking soda

½ teaspoon sea salt, plus a pinch

⅛ teaspoon ground cinnamon

115 g (4 oz) unsalted butter, softened

100 g (3½ oz) dark brown sugar

50 g (1¾ oz) granulated sugar

1 tablespoon molasses

1 large egg, at room temperature

½ teaspoon natural vanilla extract

2 egg whites

Pinch of cream of tartar

110 g (4 oz) caster (superfine) sugar

115 g (4 oz) plain chocolate, cut into 18 pieces

Sea salt, for sprinkling

makes 18   **prep** 30 mins   **cook** 20 mins

Preheat the oven to 180°C (350°F) with shelves on upper and lower third of the oven. Line 2 baking sheets with baking paper and set aside.

Combine the flours, baking powder, baking soda, the ½ teaspoon salt and cinnamon in a medium bowl and whisk to combine. Set aside.

Place the butter and brown and granulated sugars in a stand mixer fitted with a paddle attachment and cream on medium–high speed for 5 minutes, or until light and fluffy. Scrape down the bowl and reduce the speed to low. Add the molasses, egg and vanilla. Add the flour mixture on low and mix until just combined. Don't overmix.

Add the egg whites, cream of tartar and pinch of salt to a large bowl. Using a hand-held mixer on low, whisk until foamy. Add the caster sugar, 1 tablespoon at a time, until fully incorporated. Continue whisking on high for 6–8 minutes until stiff glossy peaks form. Fold the meringue into the dough, swirling a few times to still have large visible streaks. Use 2 spoons to drop 9 heaped tablespoons (40 g/1½ oz) on each prepared sheet, leaving 7.5 cm (3 in) in between each cookie. Alternatively, for a more visible swirl, scoop a heaped spoonful of meringue and a slightly smaller spoonful of the dough and swirl using the spoons after placing the dough on the sheet.

Push a piece of chocolate lightly into the top of each and bake for 10 minutes. Rotate the sheets top to bottom and back to front and bake for another 6 minutes until golden. Cool slightly on wire racks before sprinkling with sea salt.

PEACH SHISO GRANITA

Granitas are the easiest way to transform a fruit into a dessert. While many people rake the granita during the freezing process it actually works out beautifully to let it freeze solid then scrape just before serving.

---

55 g (2 oz/¼ cup) granulated sugar

Pinch of salt

8 shiso leaves

450 g (1 lb) white and yellow peaches, stoned and chopped

serves 8   **prep** 5 mins + 6 hours to cool & freeze **cook** 5 mins

Bring the sugar, salt and 240 ml (8 fl oz) water to a simmer in a small saucepan. Stir until completely dissolved, then remove from the heat. Fully submerge the shiso leaves and steep for 2 hours, or until completely cooled. Remove the leaves from the syrup.

Purée the peaches and the syrup in a blender until smooth. Transfer to a freezerproof container, such as a 20 x 20 cm (8 x 8 in) pan and freeze for 4 hours, or until completely frozen. Scrape well with a fork before serving into chilled glasses.

Note: Other fruit options include grapes, cherimoya (custard apple), persimmons and watermelon.

CALIFORNIA BAY ICE CREAM

Often only used as a supporting flavour in stocks, soups, braises or stews, fresh California bay leaves pack a punchy and bright, slightly peppery and herbal flavour that shines in this ice cream.

6 egg yolks

150 g (5½ oz) granulated sugar

355 ml (12 fl oz) double (heavy) cream

355 ml (12 fl oz) full-fat milk

5 fresh bay leaves, torn

Sea salt flakes

Honey, to serve

Extra virgin olive oil, to serve

makes 1 litre (4 cups)   **prep** 20 mins + 4 hours to cool completely & at least 4 hours to freeze   **cook** 15 mins

Freeze the bowl of an ice-cream maker overnight or according to the machine's instructions. Chill a 1.5 litre (51 fl oz/6 cup) container in the freezer to store the finished ice cream.

Whisk the egg yolks and half the sugar together in a large bowl until well combined. Set aside.

Combine the cream, milk, bay leaves, pinch of salt and the remaining sugar in a medium saucepan and heat over medium heat until hot with visible steam but not simmering, stirring frequently, to dissolve the sugar for 5 minutes. Whisking constantly, slowly stream 240 ml (8 fl oz) of the cream mixture into the egg yolk mixture. Return this mixture to the pan and over medium heat. Stir constantly with a wooden spoon until it is 82°C (180°F), about 10–15 minutes until thickened and a finger swiped across the back of the spoon leaves a clear line.

Transfer the mixture to a container and set in an ice bath to cool. Chill in the fridge for at least 4 hours, or until completely cold. Strain through a fine-mesh sieve to remove the bay leaves and cooked egg if any. Churn in the ice-cream maker according to the manufacturer's instructions. Press a piece of plastic wrap against the surface, cover and freeze for 4 hours, or until firm. Serve with a drizzle of honey, olive oil and a pinch of salt.

NUT MILK PANNA COTTA
WITH CANDIED KUMQUATS

The combination of the home-made nut milk and toasted fennel seeds lends a delicate floral flavour and the sweet tart of the candied citrus complements it so perfectly.

1½ teaspoons gelatine granules

1 tablespoon fennel seeds, lightly crushed

710 ml (24 fl oz) Nut Milk (see page 55)

75 g (2¾ oz/⅓ cup) granulated sugar

Pinch of sea salt flakes

Candied Kumquats (see page 203), fennel pollen and/or fennel flowers, to serve

serves 6   **prep** 20 mins + 6 hours chilling
cook 5 mins + 10 mins to steep

In a small bowl, sprinkle the gelatine over 2 tablespoons cold water and leave for at least 5 minutes to soften.

Toast the fennel seeds in a small saucepan over medium heat for 1 minute or until fragrant. Add the nut milk, sugar and salt and simmer, stirring until the sugar and salt have dissolved, about 2–3 minutes. Turn the heat off and leave for 10 minutes to infuse. Pour through a fine-mesh sieve into a large measuring cup or bowl.

Pour 120 ml (4 fl oz) of the nut milk into the gelatine and whisk until smooth. Return to the remaining mixture and whisk to combine. Chill in the fridge for about 2 hours, whisking every 15 minutes, until the mixture has thickened to the consistency of double (heavy) cream. Divide among 6 ramekins or glasses and chill for at least 4 hours, or overnight.

Serve topped with Candied Kumquats and a sprinkle of fennel pollen and/or fennel flowers.

STONE FRUIT SKILLET POPPYSEED CAKE

Following Californians' doctrine of eating seasonally will make this cake interesting all year long by using whatever fruits are at their peak.

110 g (4 oz) coconut oil, plus extra for greasing

125 g (4½ oz) plain (all-purpose) flour

110 g (4 oz) almond flour

1½ teaspoons baking powder

½ teaspoon baking soda

1½ teaspoons poppyseeds

½ teaspoon sea salt

100 g (3½ oz) light brown sugar

85 g (3 oz) granulated sugar

2 large eggs, at room temperature

1 teaspoon natural vanilla extract

Grated zest of 1 lemon

225 g (8 oz) sour cream, at room temperature

450 g (1 lb) summer stone fruit or other seasonal fruit, sliced

Whipped cream or ice cream, to serve (optional)

serves 8 **prep** 20 mins **cook** 45 mins

Preheat the oven to 180°C (350°F). Position a rack on the upper third of the oven. Grease a 25 cm (10 in) cast-iron frying pan and set aside.

Combine the flours, baking powder, baking soda, poppyseeds and salt in a bowl and whisk to combine. Set aside.

Place the coconut oil, brown sugar and 55 g (2 oz/¼ cup) of the granulated sugar in a stand mixer fitted with a paddle attachment and cream on medium–high speed for 3 minutes, or until light and fluffy. Scrape down the bowl and add the eggs, one at a time, scraping after each addition. Add the vanilla and lemon zest and mix for 30 seconds.

With the mixer on low, alternate adding half the dry mixture, sour cream and remaining dry mixture, scraping once. Mix only until just combined. Scrape into the prepared pan and level the top.

Arrange the fruit over the cake and sprinkle with the remaining granulated sugar. Bake for 45 minutes, or until golden and a skewer comes out clean from the middle. Leave to rest for at least 30 minutes. Serve with whipped cream or ice cream, if liked.

BASICS

These essentials will help maximise flavours in your cooking –
well worth the time and effort. Many of the preserves and
pickles make for beautiful gifts as well as utilise the abundance
of seasonal fruit and produce. Use the savoury pesto and green
goddess to eat with just about anything.

VEGETABLE STOCK

Stock is always a useful ingredient to have when needing extra flavour in a braise or stew. This recipe can also be used as a soup base for the vegetable dumplings on page 71.

---

1 celeriac (about 250 g/9 oz), peeled and cut into 6

1 swede (rutabaga) (about 115 g/4 oz)

2 parsnips (about 115 g/4 oz)

2 carrots (about 115 g/4 oz)

2 celery stalks (about 100 g/ 3½ oz), cut into thirds (if celeriac has stalks, can use in place)

8 shiitake mushrooms (about 115 g/4 oz), stems on

1 small onion, halved

1 fresh bay leaf

1 tablespoon salt

makes about 2.5 litres (85 fl oz/10 cups)
prep 5 mins   **cook** 2 hours

Place all the vegetables and bay leaf in a large saucepan. Add 5 litres (170 fl oz/20 cups) water and the salt and bring to the boil. Reduce the heat and simmer for about 2 hours, checking occasionally for small bubbles. The stock is ready when it is reduced by half and the vegetables no longer have flavour.

BONE BROTH

It's not uncommon to see people sipping broth out of a to-go cup in California. For a busy weeknight, add leftover vegetables and grains to the broth, crack an egg to poach and top with herbs or cheese for a complete meal.

---

60 ml (2 fl oz/¼ cup) extra virgin olive oil, plus extra for oiling

2.25 kg (5 lb) mixed beef bones (split marrow, oxtail, short ribs with meat)

2 celeriacs, peeled and halved

2 onions, halved

1 garlic bulb, halved crossways

1 tablespoon salt

1 bunch of thyme

2 fresh bay leaves

1 teaspoon whole black peppercorns

1 tablespoon apple cider vinegar

Sea salt flakes

makes about 2 litres (68 fl oz/8 cups) **prep** 5 mins **cook** 8 hours up to 24 hours

Preheat the oven to 240°C (465°F) and place a baking sheet on the bottom rack.

Lightly oil the baking sheet, then place the beef, celeriacs, onions and garlic on the sheet. Sprinkle with the salt and roast on the bottom rack for 30 minutes, tossing the ingredients and rotating the sheet halfway through, or until everything is browned.

Carefully transfer the beef and vegetables to a large stockpot. Use a little water and flat spatula to scrape any brown bits that have stuck to the sheet and add to the pot. Add the thyme, bay leaves, peppercorns and 3.75 litres (126½ fl oz/15 cups) water to cover. Bring to the boil and skim off any foam that rises to the top. Reduce the heat to very low, add the vinegar and simmer very gently for at least 8 hours and up to 24 hours.

Strain through a large colander lined with a muslin cloth. Cool and transfer to containers to store in the fridge for up to 5 days or freeze for 2 months. Skim the fat off once it is fully chilled. Reheat and season before using.

STRAWBERRY ROSE JAM

A good jam is the star when eaten with thick toast and salty butter, but it can also be a lovely addition to granola with yoghurt or even on top of ice cream.

1.4 kg (3 lb) strawberries, hulled and halved or quartered if large

330 g (11½ oz/1½ cups) granulated sugar

1 teaspoon sea salt flakes

½ bunch of rose geranium leaves, whole sprigs, stems and flowers (40 g/1½ oz)

2.5 cm (1 in) piece of fresh ginger, peeled and sliced

2 tablespoons lemon juice

makes 600 ml (20½ fl oz)   **prep** 10 mins
cook 15 mins

Place a few small plates in the freezer.

Place the fruit in a large saucepan. Add the sugar and salt and toss well to combine. Mash half the fruit. This will allow for a varied texture in your jam.

Wrap the rose geranium and ginger in a doubled piece of muslin cloth and tie together. Add to the pan, turn on the heat to medium–high. Cook for 15 minutes, stirring along the side and bottom of the saucepan occasionally in the beginning and more frequently towards the end of the cooking time. Spoon a little jam onto a cold plate and chill for 3 minutes. To test that the jam has thickened, run your finger or spoon through the plated jam to see that the streak does not fill back in. Stir in the lemon juice and remove the aromatic bundle.

Transfer the jams to sterilised jars and leave to cool. Seal and use within 1 month.

CANDIED KUMQUATS

Only in California do you run into the problem of having so much citrus that you see baskets of fruit in front yards with signs that say 'please take'. Candying is a great way to solve this. Add cardamom pods, fennel seeds or a little rose water for an extra touch.

---

680 g (1½ lb) whole kumquats

440 g (15½ oz/2 cups) granulated sugar

2 cardamom pods, lightly crushed

Pinch of sea salt flakes

makes 1 litre (34 fl oz/4 cups)　**prep** 5 mins
cook 1 hour

Place the kumquats in a saucepan and add the sugar, 475 ml (16 fl oz) water, cardamom and the salt. Bring to the boil, stirring occasionally to dissolve the sugar. Reduce the heat and simmer for 1 hour, or until the kumquats are translucent. Remove from the heat and leave the kumquats to cool completely in the syrup.

Transfer the kumquats and the syrup to clean jars and store in the fridge for up to 3 months. Top the panna cotta (page 191) with candied little jewels or add the syrup to iced teas (page 53) to sweeten.

Note: You can also try candying citrus peels with this method. For thicker peels, such as pomelo and grapefruit, trim away up to 3 mm (⅛ in) of pith and cut the peels into strips. Blanch the peels 2–3 times to remove the bitterness, if liked.

PASSIONFRUIT CURD

Curd is a way to use up egg yolks and is an extra special touch when serving pancakes and waffles or when filling home-made donuts (see page 183).

115 g (4 oz) butter, softened

220 g (8 oz/1 cup) granulated sugar

4 large egg yolks, at room temperature

120 ml (4 fl oz) passionfruit juice (about 6 ripe passionfruits strained of seeds), at room temperature

½ teaspoon sea salt

makes 475 ml (16 fl oz)　**prep** 10 mins　**cook** 10 mins

Place the butter and sugar in a stand mixer fitted with a paddle attachment and cream at medium–high speed for 3–4 minutes until light and fluffy. Add the egg yolks, one at a time, beating well after each addition and scraping down the side halfway through. Reduce the speed to low, add the juice and salt and mix until combined.

Transfer the mixture to a saucepan and cook over medium heat, stirring constantly and scraping down the side of the pan for 7 minutes, or until the mixture is hot with visible steam but not simmering. Pour into a heatproof jar and leave to cool to room temperature before covering and transferring to the fridge. Store for up to a month.

Serve with pancakes (see page 41) in place of maple syrup and use for donut filling (see page 183).

PESTO

Pesto can be made from any herbs, greens or a combination. Rocket (arugula) has a natural horseradish-like kick that adds a nice dimension. Switch things up with seeds, other acids and cheeses too.

85 g (3 oz) rocket (arugula) leaves

75 g (2¾ oz) raw almonds

1 small shallot, chopped

Grated zest of 1 lemon

240 ml (8 fl oz) extra virgin olive oil

100 g (3½ oz) parmesan cheese, finely grated

Sea salt flakes and freshly ground black pepper

makes 475 ml (16 fl oz) **prep** 5 mins **cook** none

Place the rocket, almonds, shallot, lemon zest, ½ teaspoon salt and ½ teaspoon pepper in a blender or food processor. Stream in the olive oil while pulsing until combined but still slightly chunky. Stir in the cheese to combine. Season to taste depending on use.

PICKLED VEGETABLES – 2 TYPES

The biggest delight in a jar of pickles is that you can use every last drop. Try the liquid in place of vinegar for salad dressings.

makes a 1 litre (34 fl oz/4 cup) jar   **prep** 5 mins   **cook** 5 mins

CRUNCHY PICKLES

370 g (13 oz) crunchy vegetables – see below

2 small shallots, finely sliced

2 garlic cloves, lightly crushed

3 herb sprigs, such as thyme, rosemary, tarragon, bay leaves and coriander (cilantro)

Fresh or dried chillies (optional)

2 tablespoons mixed whole spices, such as black peppercorns, coriander seeds, mustard seeds and celery seeds

240 ml (8 fl oz) rice vinegar

1 tablespoon granulated sugar

2 tablespoons sea salt

Crunchy vegetables:

Baby carrots

Radishes, halved if large

Beets, sliced

Summer beans

Cauliflower, cut into florets

Place the vegetables, shallots, garlic, herbs and chillies, if using, in a 1 litre (34 fl oz/4 cup) jar.

Add the whole spices to a small saucepan and toast over medium heat for 1 minute, or until fragrant. Add 240 ml (8 fl oz) water, the vinegar, sugar and salt and bring to a simmer. Whisk until the sugar and salt are just dissolved. Pour the brine over the vegetables. Cool completely before sealing. Store in the fridge for up to 3 months. While you can start eating them the following day, they will develop more flavour as they cure.

HALF SOUR PICKLES

2 tablespoons sea salt

3 garlic cloves, smashed

3 dill sprigs

1.5 cm (½ in) piece of fresh horseradish or 1 tablespoon jarred (optional)

1 teaspoon mustard seeds

1 teaspoon celery seeds

1 teaspoon black peppercorns

370 g (13 oz) pickling cucumbers, stems trimmed

Place all the ingredients except the cucumbers in a 1 litre (34 fl oz/4 cup) jar with 475 ml (16 fl oz) water. Seal and shake to dissolve. Add the cucumbers and shake to incorporate. Place in the fridge, shaking once a day.

Enjoy as early as a week but the flavours will continue to develop as they stand. After 30 days, they may start to fully cure and not be as crunchy as this style is meant to be. Great to add to potato salads (see page 127) or on burgers (see page 141).

AVOCADO GREEN GODDESS

This dressing is a take on the original from San Francisco. The creamy avocado replaces the need for sour cream or mayonnaise. It can be enjoyed thick as a dip with crudités or thinned out as a dressing.

---

1 avocado, stoned and sliced

6 anchovy fillets, drained

15 g (½ oz) parsley, leaves and tender stems

15 g (½ oz) chives

10 g (¼ oz) tarragon, leaves and tender stems

10 g (¼ oz) mint leaves

2 tablespoons extra virgin olive oil

Grated zest of 1 lemon, plus 1 tablespoon juice

1 teaspoon rice wine vinegar

Sea salt flakes and freshly ground black pepper

makes 350 ml (12 fl oz) **prep** 10 mins **cook** none

Blitz all the ingredients in a food processor until smooth and lightly flecked with green herbs, scraping down the side as necessary. Season with salt and pepper.

For a thinner dressing, add 1 tablespoon water at a time and process until you reach the desired consistency. Season lightly.

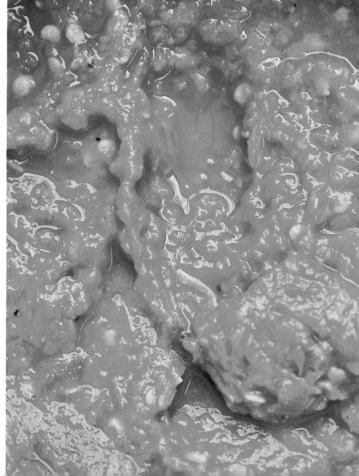

FERMENTED HOT SAUCE

A way to capture the full essence of a chilli when making hot sauce is to add a little funk from fermenting. It's similar to the depth of flavour in yeasted doughs.

1 small shallot, chopped

6 garlic cloves, smashed and skins discarded

35 g (1¼ oz) salt

10 whole black peppercorns

1 tablespoon maple syrup

340 g (12 oz) mixed red chillies

115 g (4 oz) habanero chillies

Few herb sprigs (optional)

Vinegar of choice, to taste

makes 475–710 ml (16–24 fl oz) depending on desired consistency   **prep** 10 mins + 30 days to ferment **cook** none

Place the shallot, garlic, salt, peppercorns, maple syrup and 950 ml (32 fl oz) water in a 1.9 litre (64 fl oz) jar. Seal and shake to dissolve.

Use gloves when handling chillies. Slice the mixed red chillies into rings and discard the stems. Cut the habaneros in half lengthways, seed and remove the stems, then slice. Transfer the chillies and herbs, if using, to the jar. Cover with the lid and leave in a cool spot on a work surface out of direct sunlight. Open the lid daily to burp the jar (allows gas build-up to release) then stir or shake lightly. Repeat for 30 days. Bubbles may lessen as the ferment continues.

When ready, strain and save the fermenting liquid. Place the vegetables in a blender and process until desired consistency, adding 1 tablespoon of the reserved liquid at a time to get the sauce going. For a chunky hot sauce, pulse until ideal texture. For a thick sauce, purée until smooth. For a thin hot sauce, purée until smooth, adding additional liquid a little at a time. Check for flavour balance and add vinegar of choice, if liked. Store in small sterilised jars for up to 3 months in the fridge.

HERB & FLORAL ICE CUBES

Freeze left-over fragrant herbs or edible flowers into ice cubes to add extra flavour and beauty into cocktails, iced teas or morning shakes. This way, nothing goes to waste.

25–50 g (1–1¾ oz) edible flowers or small floral herbs

Herb & flower options:

Wood sorrel and flowers

Regular sorrel

Mint

Coriander (cilantro) leaves and flowers

Rocket (arugula) flowers

Lemon verbena

Dill

Borage flowers

Flowering sage

Rose geranium

makes 2 trays of ice cubes **prep** 5 mins + 4 hours to freeze **cook** none

Divide the flowers or herbs into 2 ice trays and fill with filtered water. Freeze for 4 hours, or until frozen.

PRESERVED CITRUS

Walking through Californian neighbourhoods in the winter, pavements are littered with fallen fruit. Preserving is a great way to use up the entire fruit. Try the preserved lemons with the Crispy Chicken with Beans (page 147) or Lemony Burrata Flatbread (page 113).

---

70 g (2½ oz) sea salt

3 tablespoons granulated sugar

1 tablespoon mixed spices, such as pink peppercorns, fennel and coriander seeds

680 g (1½ lb) meyer lemons (about 8 small), well scrubbed

3 fresh bay leaves

VARIATIONS:

Citrus: mixed variety lemons, limes, Persian limes, oranges, mandarins, kumquats

Whole spices: black, white or green peppercorns, caraway, cumin, cardamom, star anise, cinnamon, clove

Hearty herbs: thyme, rosemary, savory

Dried whole chilli

makes a 1 litre (34 fl oz/4 cup) jar
prep 5 mins + 30 days to cure   **cook** none

Combine the salt, sugar and whole spices together in a small bowl. Place 1 tablespoon of the mixture in a clean 1 litre (34 fl oz/4 cup) jar.

Quarter each lemon almost all the way through while leaving one end intact. Open each like a flower and rub the salt mix inside, then on the rind. Place half in the jar, pushing down. Add bay leaves halfway through. Continue with the remaining lemons. Top with the rest of the salt mix. Leave in a cool spot for 30 days, shaking daily. Chill for up to 6 months. Rinse before using. Chop or slice rind. Juice can be used in dressings. Flesh can be added to marinades or stews.

RECIPE LIST

INDEX

SUPPLIERS

Thank you to all the people, businesses and incredible experiences that inspired this book and brought it to life.

FERRY PLAZA FARMERS' MARKET
1 Ferry Building
San Francisco, CA 94111
001.415.291.3276
www.cuesa.org
Tuesday, Thursday, Saturday

FINLEY FARMS
1702 N Refugio Rd
Santa Ynez, CA 93460
001.805.686.0209
finleyfarmsorganic@gmail.com

GARCIA ORGANIC FARM
Juan & Coco Garcia
40430 De Luz Murrieta Road
Murrieta, CA 92563
001.760.728.5925
@garciaorganicfarm

HAWKINS NEW YORK
767 S Alameda Street, Los Angeles, CA
613 Warren Street, Hudson, New York
17 8th Avenue, NY, New York
001.844.HNY.3344
www.hawkinsnewyork.com

HOG ISLAND OYSTER CO.
20215 Shoreline Highway
Marshall, CA 94940
001.415.663.9218
www.hogislandoysters.com

PASCAL BAUDAR
www.urbanoutdoorskills.com
www.instagram.com/pascalbaudar/

PROPLINK
2301 E 7th Street, Suite A101
Los Angeles, CA 90023
001.323.763.3236
www.proplinkla.com

SANTA MONICA FARMERS' MARKET
Arizona Avenue at 2nd Street on Wednesday
Arizona Avenue at 3rd Street on Saturday
001.310.458-8411
www.smgov.net/portals/farmersmarket/

SCRIBE WINERY
2100 Denmark Street
Sonoma, CA 95476
001.707.939.1858
www.scribewinery.com

STRONG ARM FARM
Heidi Herrmann
strongarmfarm@gmail.com
Book seaweed forage classes through
www.foragesf.com/seaweed-foraging

TOTEM HOME
info@totemhome.com
www.totemhome.com

ACKNOWLEDGEMENTS

Thank you to Catie Ziller at Marabout for the encouragement and opportunity to make a beautiful book. To Con Poulos, thank you for your talent and incredible efforts. Your ability to capture the beauty in everything is unparalleled. To Cybelle Tondu, I am incredibly thankful for all your help with this book. Your diligence in and outside the kitchen is exceptional. To Katherine Knowlton, thank you for all your hard work. You are a joy to have in the kitchen. Thank you Brett Regot for your invaluable input and testing. Thank you Kathy Steer for your energy and care in the laborious book edits. To Alice Chadwick, thank you for the design and creativity on this project. Finally, thank you Mark for your unconditional support and patience.

First published in French by Hachette Livre (Marabout) in 2019

This edition published in 2020 by Smith Street Books

Naarm | Melbourne | Australia | smithstreetbooks.com

ISBN: 978-1-925811-66-7

Publisher (Smith Street Books): Paul McNally

Publisher (Marabout): Catie Ziller

Author & food stylist: Vivian Lui

Photographer: Con Poulos

Food stylist assistants: Cybelle Tondu & Katherine Knowlton

Design & illustrations: Alice Chadwick

Project editor: Kathy Steer

Printed & bound in China

Book 132

10 9 8 7 6 5 4 3 2 1